DARK
AGENDA

DARK AGENDA

The War to Destroy Christian America

DAVID HOROWITZ

Humanix Books
www.humanixbooks.com

Humanix Books

Dark Agenda
Copyright © 2018 by David Horowitz
All rights reserved

Humanix Books, P.O. Box 20989, West Palm Beach, FL 33416, USA
www.humanixbooks.com | info@humanixbooks.com

Library of Congress Cataloging-in-Publication Data is available upon request.

Humanix Books is a division of Humanix Publishing, LLC. Its trademark, consisting of the word "Humanix," is registered in the Patent and Trademark Office and in other countries.

ISBN: 978-163006-114-2 (Hardcover)
ISBN: 978-163006-113-5 (E-book)

Printed in the United States of America
10 9 8 7 6 5 4 3 2 1

To April

For making these years

the happiest of my life,

and

To my Christian buddies,

Peter, Wally, and Mike

for making me a better man

The establishment of Civil and Religious Liberty was the Motive which induced me to the Field, the object is obtained, and it now remains to be my earnest wish and prayer, that the Citizens of the United States would make a wise and virtuous use of the blessings, placed before them.

—GEORGE WASHINGTON, 1783

Contents

Acknowledgments

I WANT TO THANK CHRIS Ruddy for coming up with the idea for this book and choosing me to write it; and John Perazzo, Elizabeth Ruiz, and Sara Dogan for helping me to research it. Jim Denney did yeoman's work as an editor, not only keeping the author honest, but making his prose more accessible to others, while providing choice anecdotes that made this book's argument clearer and more powerful.

1

Religion Must Die

On Sunday morning, November 5, 2017, a gunman walked into the First Baptist Church in Sutherland Springs, Texas. He wore tactical gear and a black face mask marked with a white skull, and he carried a semiautomatic rifle. He shot and killed two people outside the church, then went inside, walking up and down the aisle, cursing and shooting people in the pews. He reloaded again and again, emptying fifteen magazines of ammunition.

When the gunman emerged from the church, he found an armed citizen facing him from across the street—a former NRA firearms instructor named Stephen Willeford. The two men exchanged fire, and Willeford hit the gunman in the leg and upper body. The wounded shooter limped to his car and sped away. He was later found at the wheel of his crashed car, killed by a self-inflicted gunshot to the head.

The attack killed twenty-six people, ages five to seventy-two, and wounded twenty. The killer had been court-martialed in the Air Force for domestic violence (he had beaten his wife and cracked the skull of his infant stepson). The Air Force failed to report his conviction to the FBI's crime information database.

The slaughter of unarmed Christians in a church sanctuary was a cowardly attack on one church. But what happened *after* the church shooting was part of a wider war by the political left against Christians and Christianity.

As news of the shooting broke, prominent Christians took to Twitter and urged fellow believers to pray. Speaker of the House Paul Ryan, a devout Roman Catholic, tweeted, "Reports out of Texas are devastating. The people of Sutherland Springs need our prayers right now."

From Hollywood to New York and Washington, the left responded with a chorus of jeers and insults. Former MSNBC political commentator Keith Olbermann suggested in a tweet that Speaker Ryan should proctologize himself with his prayers. Seattle Democrat, Representative Pramila Jayapal, tweeted, "They were praying when it happened. They don't need our prayers. They need us to address gun violence . . . ." Comedian Paula Poundstone sneered: "If prayers were the answer" to mass shootings, "wouldn't people at a church service be safe?" Actor Wil Wheaton tweeted, "The murdered victims were in a church. If prayers did anything, they'd still be alive, you worthless sack of . . . ."

These and other comments from the secular left displayed not only a smug disdain for Christians but an amazing ignorance of how religious Christians view prayer. Christians don't view prayer as a magic incantation to make themselves bulletproof. Christians believe in the teachings of Christ who warned them: "In the world ye shall have tribulation." In the Garden of Gethsemane Christ prayed to be delivered from the agony of the cross, but he ended his prayer, "nevertheless not my will, but thine, be done." The answer to Christ's prayer was silence—and he was later crucified on a Roman cross.

In her commentary on the church shooting, MSNBC host Joy-Ann Reid tweeted that "when Jesus of Nazareth came upon thousands of hungry people," he didn't pray; he fed the people. She's simply wrong. Matthew 14:19 records that, before Jesus fed the people, he looked heavenward and prayed. Jesus prayed *and* he acted. That's how his followers still view prayer. They pray *and* they act. At around the same time Joy-Ann Reid was tweeting, the Billy Graham Rapid Response Team was already in action, rolling into Sutherland Springs with sixteen chaplains to comfort grieving families and help meet their material needs. Two days after the shooting, the Southern Baptist Convention announced it would pay all funeral expenses for the twenty-six slain churchgoers.

Because this is a world made by flawed human beings, it will continue to be a world of tribulations. There will be more shootings, attacks, fires, floods, earthquakes, and other tragedies. Christians will call for prayer, and leftists will mock them for it, imagining there are solutions that can perfect this life, and regarding Christians as the enemies of that perfection.

The War

Since its birth in the fires of the French Revolution, the political left has been at war with religion, and with the Christian religion in particular. In a symbolic revolutionary act, the Jacobin leaders of the French Revolution changed the name of the Cathedral of Notre Dame to the "Temple of Reason." Then, in the name of "reason," they proceeded to massacre the inhabitants of the Vendée region of west central France because its citizens were Catholics.

This has been called the first modern genocide, but it was far from the last. Karl Marx famously described religion as "the opium of the people" and "the sigh of the oppressed." Inspired by his hatred ever since, revolutionaries have regarded religion as the enemy of progress and the mask of oppression. In Russia, Marx's disciples removed religious teaching from the schools, outlawed criticism of atheists and agnostics, and burned 100,000 churches. When priests demanded freedom of religion, they were sentenced to death. Between 1917 and 1935, 130,000 Russian Orthodox priests were arrested, 95,000 of whom were executed by firing squad.[1]

Radicals in America today don't have the political power to execute religious people and destroy their houses of worship. Yet they openly declare their desire to obliterate religion. In their own minds, their intentions are noble—they want to save the human race from the social injustice and oppression that religion allegedly inflicts on humanity.

"Religion must die in order for mankind to live," proclaimed left-wing commentator and comedian Bill Maher in *Religulous*, the most-watched documentary feature of 2008.

Both title and script were transparent attempts to stigmatize religious people as dangerous morons whose views could not be taken seriously. Throughout the film, Maher travels to Jerusalem, the Vatican, and Salt Lake City, as well as other centers of religion, interviewing believers and making them appear foolish. How did he gain interviews with his victims? He lied to them, saying he was making a film called *A Spiritual Journey*.[2]

According to Maher, "The irony of religion is that because of its power to divert man to destructive courses, the world could actually come to an end." He predicts the destruction of the human race as a result of "religion-inspired nuclear terrorism." Hence the need for religion to die if mankind is to live. Maher's views accurately reflect the attitudes of a movement called the "New Atheism," whose leaders are prominent scientists and best-selling authors, far superior in intellect to Maher but equally contemptuous of religion and religious believers. Like Maher's film, the New Atheism movement seeks to discredit all religious belief by caricaturing its adherents as simpletons, and worse. The stated goal of the New Atheism is to delegitimize and extinguish the religious point of view.

Maher's suggestion that religion—and evidently religion alone—threatens the existence of the human race is simply malicious. Both he and the New Atheists are blind to all the positive influences religion has had on human behavior, and they ignore all the atheist-inspired genocides of the last 250 years. In the twentieth century alone, Communist atheists slaughtered more than 100 million people in Russia, China, and Indochina. Not even the bloodthirsty jihadists of radical Islam have killed innocents on anything close to such a scale.

It's striking that Maher and the New Atheists ignore the appalling body count of Marxism—an ideology that is explicitly atheistic, whose atrocities were committed in the name of social justice. According to Maher it is religious people who are "irrationalists," and dangerous because they "steer the ship of state not by a compass, but by the equivalent of reading the entrails of a chicken." Yet civilization was built and improved by such irrationalists—believers like Locke, Newton, Washington, Wilberforce, Sojourner Truth, and Abraham Lincoln. For the five millennia of recorded history, with few exceptions the most rational, compassionate, and successful decision makers, both military and civilian, have been people guided by a belief in God, including some whose spiritual compass took the form of reading the entrails of a chicken.

Near the end of Maher's rant, he pauses to address any religionist who may have unwittingly strayed into the cinema where *Religulous* was playing: "Look in the mirror and realize that the solace and comfort that religion brings you actually comes at a terrible price. If you belonged to a political party or a social club that was tied to as much bigotry, misogyny, homophobia, violence, and sheer ignorance as religion is, you'd resign in protest."

How myopic! And the crimes and horrors committed by atheism? From the French Revolution to the Bolshevik, from the Vendée to Vietnam, the bigotries and atrocities committed by the forces of godlessness match and even outweigh those committed by the forces of godliness. If a history of violence, persecution, and murder serves to discredit an ideology, why hasn't Maher resigned in protest from the party of atheism?

The New Atheists

The New Atheism arose in response to the attacks of 9/11, when Islamist jihadists, crying "Allah is great," murdered 3,000 innocents in the World Trade Center. The 9/11 attacks were indeed a case of religious fanaticism leading to heinous results. In their wake, the New Atheists to their credit, and virtually alone among progressives, did not shrink from connecting the attacks to Islamic beliefs.

They did not, however, limit their attacks to Islamic fanaticism, but maliciously included modern Christianity and Judaism in their screeds about religious terrorism. They did so despite the fact that Jews and Christians are the primary targets and victims of the Islamic jihadists. Moreover, Judaism and Christianity have undergone reformations and, as a result, have not prosecuted religious wars since the time of the Crusades.

The principal manifesto of the New Atheist movement was published in 2006. Written by evolutionary biologist Richard Dawkins, *The God Delusion* maintains that post-Darwinian scientific advances have rendered any belief in God irrational and unnecessary. To make the case, Dawkins's argument drastically narrows the compass of religious teachings, viewing them as crude and fallacy-ridden attempts to provide nonscientific accounts of natural forces and phenomena.

But how many Jews and Christians today actually cling to a literal reading of the Bible? How many go to church or synagogue to challenge the knowledge that science has provided of the workings of the universe? Dr. Jennifer Wiseman is a devout Christian and the senior astrophysicist (with degrees from MIT and Harvard) at NASA's Goddard Space Flight Center. She said, "You have to look at biblical literature from the perspective of when it was written, the original audiences, the original languages, the original purposes... the message that was meant to be conveyed by it. The Bible's not a science text."[3]

In attacking religious people for their ignorance of science, Richard Dawkins fails to account for the many scientists who, like Wiseman, are religious, who believe in a Divinity, and who see no conflict between faith and science. He also dismisses the spiritual and moral dimensions of religion—perhaps its most important features. Do the profound moral lessons of Genesis depend on thinking the world was created 6,000 years ago, in six 24-hour days? If Genesis were a work of fiction, it would still provide believers and nonbelievers with guides to a better life.

The most telling aspect of Dawkins's argument is the unscientific *animus* with which it is pursued. The vitriol that infuses his book suggests an agenda that is not wholly, or even primarily, intellectual: "The God of the Old Testament is arguably the most unpleasant character in all fiction: jealous and proud of it; a petty, unjust, unforgiving control-freak; a vindictive, bloodthirsty ethnic cleanser; a misogynistic, homophobic, racist, infanticidal, genocidal, filicidal, pestilential, megalomaniacal, sadomasochistic, capriciously malevolent bully."[4]

Only a fool would worship such a God. But consider, for a moment, the particulars of Dawkins's indictment. "Megalomaniacal" means to have delusions of grandeur. If God is God, then His grandeur is hardly a delusion. "Control freak"? If God is the Author of everything, then isn't "control" implicit in His job description? And how can "control freak" be applied to Him except by a comedian in search of a laugh line? "Pestilential"? Can Dawkins be referring to the locusts, which Exodus describes as a plague designed to free His people from slavery in Egypt? Is Dawkins siding with the Egyptian slave masters? Or is he misreading a story that might be metaphorical or that actually contains some historical facts?

Dawkins's writing oozes contempt for people of faith:

> Do we know of any... examples where stupid ideas have been known to spread like an epidemic? Yes, by God! Religion. Religious ideas are irrational. Religious beliefs are dumb and dumber: super dumb. Religion drives otherwise sensible people into celibate monasteries, or crashing into New York skyscrapers. Religion motivates people to whip their own backs, to set fire to themselves or their daughters, to denounce their own grandmothers as witches, or, in less extreme cases, simply to stand or kneel, week after week, through ceremonies of stupefying boredom.[5]

The idea that all religious people are stupid is, well, stupid. Of course there are dumb religious people, just as there are dumb nonreligious people. However, both Isaac Newton and Galileo were devout Christians, as were virtually all the geniuses who created the scientific revolutions we associate with the Enlightenment, from Galileo to Pascal. In fact, they were inspired to look for order in the universe precisely because they believed it was the work of a Divine designer.

A Dialogue Between Science and Faith

A contemporary example of a devoutly believing scientist is Dr. Francis Collins, who headed the Human Genome Project from 1993 to 2008 and is currently the director of the National Institutes of Health (NIH). He once wrote, "I have found there is a wonderful harmony in the complementary truths of science and faith. The God of the Bible is also the God of the genome. God can be found in the cathedral or in the laboratory. By investigating God's majestic and awesome creation, science can actually be a means of worship."[6]

Dr. Collins is not only a believer, but a former atheist who converted to Christianity as an adult. In 2006, the same year Dawkins's book appeared, Collins published *The Language of God: A Scientist's Evidence for Belief*, which explains the compatibility of science and religious conviction. To mark the publication of both men's works, *Time International* organized a debate between them.[7] In their discussion, Collins maintained that if God is a being outside nature, then God—along with the questions pertaining to God—is outside the scope of science as well, including the question of whether God exists or not.

Collins pointed out that believers have varying views on the Genesis account of creation:

There are sincere believers who interpret *Genesis* 1 and 2 in a very literal way that is inconsistent, frankly, with our knowledge of the universe's age or of how living organisms are related to each other. St. Augustine wrote that basically it is not possible to understand what was being described in *Genesis*. It was not intended as a science textbook. It was intended as a description of who God was, who we are and what our relationship is supposed to be with God. Augustine explicitly warns against a very narrow perspective that will put our faith at risk of looking ridiculous. If you step back from that one narrow interpretation, what the Bible describes is very consistent with the Big Bang.

Dawkins and Collins did agree that science is the only valid way to explain the processes, laws, and phenomena of the natural world. "The difference," Collins said, "is that my presumption of the possibility of God and therefore the supernatural is not zero, and yours is."[8]

Another difference between the two scientists was Dawkins's ill-concealed contempt for religious people. In response to Collins's comments about those who interpret Genesis literally, Dawkins remarked that Collins would "save himself an awful lot of trouble if he just simply ceased to give them the time of day. Why bother with these clowns?"

"Richard," Collins replied, "I think we don't do a service to dialogue between science and faith to characterize sincere people by calling them names. . . . Atheists sometimes come across as a bit arrogant in this regard, and characterizing faith as something only an idiot would attach themselves to is not likely to help your case."

So why do Richard Dawkins and his fellow New Atheists demonstrate such hatred and loathing toward religious people? It's because they have a faith of their own. They see themselves as liberators—pioneers of a new millennium for the human race. They envision a future in which religion has been vanquished and rationality prevails. They want a world in which humanity is finally free from myths and superstitions. They believe in a vision of a world of "new men and women," liberated from the chains of the past. Science will usher in a utopian age of reason, enlightenment, and social justice.

This is the vision of an earthly redemption. It's a fantasy in which human beings aspire to act as gods and create new worlds—and it is nothing new. It is the faith of Marxists and Communists who set out to transform the world from the one we know into one that is entirely different—liberated. It is the essence of the original sin recorded in Genesis, when Satan tempted the first man and woman, saying, "Then your eyes shall be opened, and ye shall be as gods."[9] And it is the source of the monstrous catastrophes of the twentieth century, which were engineered by socialists in Germany and the Communist bloc.

2

Roots of the War

I FIRST MET CHRISTOPHER HITCHENS—THE most articulate and entertaining of the New Atheists—when we were both radicals in London in the 1960s. We became antagonists in the 1980s, after he immigrated to the United States and I met him again in Berkeley. By then I was a budding ex-radical, who had cast off his Marxist blinders. When Christopher shifted gears in 2001 and became a supporter of America's war against Islamic jihadists in Iraq, he came under heavy fire from his leftist comrades, and I defended him. In the last years of his life, I became his friend. These were the years of Christopher's crusade against God, which I thought was terribly misguided. Our friendship, however, was focused on other things.

Christopher's atheism (or "anti-theism," a term he considered more assertively hostile to a belief in God than mere atheism) seemed a natural outgrowth of his contrarian personality. In 2002, Christopher took part in an online chat with the UK's *Independent* paper. A reader asked him, "What do you consider to be the 'axis of evil'?" This was a reference to President Bush's characterization of three terrorist countries—Iran, Iraq, and North Korea. Christopher's reply: "Christianity, Judaism, Islam—the three leading monotheisms." It was characteristically pugnacious and perverse.

On May 1, 2007, Christopher published an atheist jeremiad—*God Is Not Great: How Religion Poisons Everything*. It stormed onto the best-seller lists, debuting at number two on Amazon (behind *Harry Potter and the Deathly Hallows*). By its third week in print, *God Is Not Great* dominated the *New York Times* best-seller list. Here's a succinct expression of the book's thesis: "Violent, irrational, intolerant, allied to racism and tribalism and bigotry, invested in ignorance and hostile to free inquiry, contemptuous of women and coercive toward children: organized religion ought to have a great deal on its conscience."[1]

With the publication of *God Is Not Great*, Christopher became the most celebrated spokesman for the New Atheism. In the final chapter he hailed the prospect of a rational future without God, calling it a "New Enlightenment."

"Religion has run out of justifications," he claimed, adding:

Thanks to the telescope and the microscope, it no longer offers explanations of anything important. . . . Meanwhile, confronted with undreamed-of vistas inside our own evolving cortex, in the farthest reaches of the known universe, and in the proteins and acids which constitute our nature, religion offers either annihilation in the name of god, or the false promise that if we take a knife to our foreskins, or pray in the right direction, or ingest pieces of wafer, we shall be "saved."[2]

In contrast to what he saw as a superstitious con game of religious belief, Christopher envisioned a "scientific progress, un-constricted by religious manacles." In this utopia, scientific progress would make possible "the divorce between the sexual life and fear, and the sexual life and disease, and the sexual life and tyranny, [which] can now at last be attempted, on the sole condition that we banish all religions from the discourse. And all this, and more, is for the first time in our history, within the reach if not the grasp of everyone."

Christopher's vision of mankind's liberation from timeless afflictions—fear, disease, tyranny—is as head-spinning as any flourish in Marx's writings. It is in fact an updated version of Christopher's lifelong romance with Marxism, which he never really abandoned.[3] Early in *God Is Not Great*, he quotes Karl Marx's famous (and widely misquoted and misunderstood) passage from the *Contribution to the Critique of Hegel's Philosophy of Right*:

Religious distress is at the same time the expression of real distress and also the *protest* against real distress. Religion is the sigh of the oppressed creature, the heart of a heartless world, just as it is the spirit of spiritless conditions. It is the opium of the people.

To abolish religion as the illusory happiness of the people is to demand their real happiness.

Like Marx, Christopher saw religion as both the oppressor of the people and the means by which people anesthetized the pain of their oppression. I did not support Christopher's antireligious fervor, because I no longer believed in a life in this world without tribulations. Christopher's failure to free himself from this Marxist illusion saddened me. I was dismayed by the way he wasted his talents on a futile war against God. Actually it was only a war against the *idea* of God, since neither Christopher nor anyone else can know as a fact whether God exists or not.

In June 2010, while in New York on a promotional tour for a memoir he named *Hitch-22*, Christopher collapsed and was rushed to the hospital. There he was diagnosed with esophageal cancer—the same aggressive cancer that had killed his father. Christopher was candid about his heavy use of alcohol and tobacco, along with his genetic predisposition, being the likely cause of his cancer. He knew he had little hope of remission. The cancer was diagnosed at stage four, and as he grimly pointed out, there is no stage five. Yet he faced his illness squarely and without self-pity or complaint.

I learned of Christopher's diagnosis as I was completing an essay called "The Two Christophers," about the contradictions in Christopher's thinking and his life—contradictions he fully and knowingly embraced. (One was his loathing of totalitarian oppression combined with his continuing affair with Marxism, which always leads to totalitarian oppression.) The news of his illness triggered memories of watching him chain-smoke while downing glass after glass of scotch. I'd think, *My friend is killing himself.* Yet no words of mine could have altered his habits.

For a week or so after learning of Christopher's diagnosis, I delayed the decision of whether to publish the piece or not. It was candid and critical of him in some respects, yet I was confident that Christopher wouldn't take offense. If ever a man appreciated blunt candor, whether on the dishing out or the receiving end, it was my friend Christopher. Yet as he was enthralled in a life-and-death medical crisis, I didn't want to make his struggle more difficult.

Finally, on July 7, 2010, I decided to publish the piece, but I wanted to show it to him first. I e-mailed it with a note that read, in part, "Some of it is critical, as you would expect. When all is said and done, however, my heart is with you. I am grieved that this misfortune has befallen you, and I look to you to pull yourself through it and get on with your journey."

He wrote back the same day—and from his reply, I realized he had misunderstood something in the piece, was hurt by it, and had stopped reading at page 2. I wrote back and explained the misunderstanding. He appreciated the clarification and added, "I am not reading well enough to distinguish commas from semi-colons." He never told me if he ever finished reading what I had written.

Three weeks later, on July 29, I e-mailed him to say I would soon be in Washington, D.C., where he lived. Would he be available for a visit from a friend? He replied, "I'd like that very much. Can you try me nearer the time? I have a rather fluctuating condition. Hope to coincide. Christopher."

We never did "coincide." When I arrived in Washington, I called him, but he was too ill to receive visitors.

Christopher died on December 15, 2011, at age 62 in a state-of-the-art cancer center in Houston, Texas. I was deeply saddened at the news. He had been struck down at the height of his intellectual powers, and died without relenting in his war against God, and consequently without devoting himself to the end-of-life reflections, and bondings, that are proper "last things."

Christopher's anti-God campaign was based on a fundamental error reflected in the subtitle of his book: *How Religion Poisons Everything*. On the contrary, since religion, as practiced, is a human activity, the reverse is true. Human beings poison religion, imposing their prejudices, superstitions, and corruptions onto its rituals and texts, not the other way around.

"Pascal Is a Fraud!"

When I first became acquainted with Christopher's crusade, I immediately thought of the seventeenth-century scientist and mathematician, Blaise Pascal. In addition to major contributions to scientific knowledge, Pascal produced exquisite reflections on religious themes:

> When I consider the short duration of my life, swallowed up in the eternity before and after, the space which I fill, and even can see, engulfed in the infinite immensity of spaces of which I am ignorant and which know me not, I am frightened and astonished at being here rather than there; for there

is no reason why here rather than there, why now rather than then. Who has put me here?⁴

These are the questions that only a religious faith can attempt to answer. There is no science of the *why* of our existence, no scientific counsel or solace for our human longings, loneliness, and fear. Without a God to make sense of our existence, Pascal wrote, human life is intolerable:

> This is what I see and what troubles me. I look on all sides, and I see only darkness everywhere. Nature presents to me nothing which is not a matter of doubt and concern. If I saw nothing there that revealed a Divinity, I would come to a negative conclusion; if I saw everywhere the signs of a Creator, I would remain peacefully in faith. But seeing too much to deny and too little to be sure, I am in a state to be pitied....⁵

To resolve this dilemma, Pascal devised his famous "wager," which, simply stated, is that since we cannot know whether there is a God or not, it is better to wager that there is one, rather than that there is not.

Could a reasoned argument like this inspire a religious faith? Pascal knew it could not. In an even more famous passage, he wrote, "The heart has its reasons, which reason does not know." His scientific head may have been skeptical, but Pascal was not. "Faith," he said, "is God felt by the heart."⁶

Pascal was a poignant figure. In ill health his entire life, by the time he reached the age of thirty-five, he was in such physical pain he had to suspend his intellectual efforts.

He withdrew from the world and gave his possessions to the poor.

In June 1662, he took in a homeless family. Soon after their arrival, members of the family showed symptoms of smallpox. Rather than put them back on the street, Pascal left his house and moved in with his brother. Shortly after the move, Pascal was seized with a violent illness. On August 19, he went into convulsions and died. He was thirty-nine years old. The last words he uttered were: "May God never abandon me."[7]

Because of my acquaintance with figures like Pascal, I winced at Christopher's attacks on religious people, calling them vermin and referring collectively to them as a plague.[8] Still, I was curious to confront him in person to see how far his anger would go and how far he was able to see around it. One California afternoon we had lunch together in the Polo Lounge at the Beverly Hills Hotel. After some hesitation, I asked him what he thought of Pascal.

"Pascal is a fraud!" he bellowed, ending the conversation.

Christopher's Faith

Mercifully, Christopher was not the ferocious caricature he often presented himself to be. He was, by his own account, a Janus figure. Janus (after whom the month of January is named) was the Roman god of doorways and duality. He was depicted as having two faces, one looking to the future, one to the past. Christopher's personality was a similar duality, often looking two ways at once.

When Christopher was in his polemical mode on the debating stage, he was an undisputed master of eloquent nastiness. But offstage, in small gatherings or private conversations, he was frequently quite gracious and charming—even toward religious people.

When Christopher was stricken with the cancer that would soon kill him, a man he had fiercely debated reached out to him. That man was Dr. Francis Collins (mentioned earlier in Chapter 1), the noted Christian geneticist and author of *The Language of God: A Scientist Presents Evidence for Belief*. Collins offered Christopher the most advanced immunotherapy available, based on an analysis of his personal genome, and Christopher turned to this believer in the hope that Collins could save his life.

Despite their opposing views on God and religion, the two men became close friends during Christopher's treatment. Christopher said, "It is a rather wonderful relationship. I won't say he doesn't pray for me, because I think he probably does; but he doesn't discuss it with me."[9] Though their friendship succeeded, the therapy failed.

The ecumenical side of Christopher was captured in a touching memoir by Larry Taunton, an evangelical Christian who drove him on his last journeys to the public occasions where he debated believers and, before large audiences, denied the existence of God. Christopher and Taunton became friends and had many cordial conversations about theology and religion. Christopher even allowed Taunton to lead him in a Bible study of the New Testament's Gospel of John.

Taunton's memoir is called *The Faith of Christopher Hitchens: The Restless Soul of the World's Most Notorious Atheist*. It recounts their discussions along the way to the debates. Their conversations reveal Christopher's ability (especially when he was offstage) to discuss religious beliefs seriously and civilly.

When the book was published after Christopher's death, it was savagely attacked by Christopher's political friends. They thought the title implied that Christopher had experienced a deathbed conversion. It was an idea Taunton explicitly denied in the book (which his detractors hadn't bothered to read). Taunton wrote:

> For me, the debates, the late-night discussions, and the Bible studies conducted in the front seat of my car were never about winning or losing an argument. Let the bloggers and the people in online forums fight that out. . . . I didn't need Christopher's conversion to feel good about myself or to reinforce a flagging faith in the claims of Jesus Christ. I have never doubted them. No, for me it was always about the struggle for his soul because I believe this verse: "I am the resurrection, and the life: he that believeth in me, though he were dead, yet shall he live."[10]

Did Christopher have a faith? Of course he did. First, he had a faith that God did not exist, something that he could not know and that science could not prove. But beyond that he had a more powerful belief in an earthly redemption, which religious people were obstructing.

Like other New Atheist romantics, Christopher was inspired by a revolutionary faith—in the transformation of humankind. When his original belief in the socialist future waned, he replaced it with a faith that reason would become the foundation of a humane world. He spent his dwindling strength and the closing days of his life in a last crusade against what he saw as superstitious, reactionary beliefs that kept people from entering this promised land.

"Through a Glass Darkly"

So what do we learn from the argument between believers and atheists? In my view, not much, since the question of whether God exists cannot be resolved. Both sides must rely on faith.

What if the atheists are right and God is a fiction? When it comes to the moral and spiritual issues that are the heart and soul of religious belief, does it matter whether religious people believe in a fiction?

Ironically, arguments made by Christopher and Richard Dawkins suggest that it matters not at all. Both concede that there are attributes of religion that many people want and need and that science cannot supply. Both then suggest that literature and the arts can provide a moral equivalent of religious faith. In Christopher's words:

> Authors as diverse as Matthew Arnold and George Orwell have given thought to the serious question: what is to be done about morals and ethics now that religion has so much decayed? Arnold went almost as far as to propose that the study of literature replace religion. I must say that I slightly dread the effect that this might have had on literary pursuit, but as a source of ethical reflection, and as a mirror in which to see our human dilemmas reflected, the literary tradition is infinitely superior to the childish parables and morality tales, let alone the sanguinary and sectarian admonitions of the "holy" books.[11]

In other words, Christopher suggests that the moral and spiritual guidance offered by the "fictions" of religion can be replaced by the superior fictions of literature. But if the atheist argument is reduced to the dubious claim that literary fictions are superior to religious ones, the whole nature of the debate has changed. It is no longer a debate about science versus religion, but about the effects of one form of storytelling versus another.

Human beings have turned to the Bible's stories for insight and guidance for thousands of years, making it hard to argue that they are not more powerful and compelling. A story backed by faith in a God who has answers to the great *why* questions will be more comforting and compelling than a story whose answers the author acknowledges are made up.

For the same reason, a story backed by religious faith can be more dangerous than a work of fiction, as Christopher and his colleagues never tire of pointing out. But religious thinkers don't deny the horrors perpetrated in the name of God. Here is Pascal's word on the subject: "Men never commit evil so fully and joyfully as when they do it for religious convictions."[12] This is true, but it's not a reason to condemn religious belief. The danger lies in human nature and the fact that human beings can poison religion and pervert its purposes.

My own theological views are those of an agnostic—one who doesn't know. I do not know whether there is a Divine designer or not. As an agnostic, what impresses me first of all is the woeful limits of our human knowledge. I respect the power of reason, but I also respect those aspects of religious faith that are compassionate and consoling. Many people could not live their lives without the consolation of faith. The virtues of religion should not be dismissed lightly.

The Christian testament has a beautiful phrase for our limited human understanding: "For now we see through a glass darkly, but then face to face: now I know in part; but then shall I know even as also I am known."[13]

Believers trust the biblical promise that all our questions will be answered when we meet God face-to-face in eternity. That promise is the heart of religious faith. For an agnostic, that promise is a reminder that our knowledge in this life is incomplete. We are well into the twenty-first century, and we marvel at the spectacular achievements of science. But science still does not know how the universe was created or how life began.

The Book of Proverbs contains a warning that speaks to us in our uncertain state: "Pride goeth before destruction, and a haughty spirit before a fall."[14] Those who believe they are changing the world, or saving the planet, or transforming the human race, are intoxicated with self-aggrandizing pride. As secular "redeemers," a haughty spirit is their second nature. Consequently, they are deaf to this biblical wisdom.

The secularists are confident that the nonexistence of God is a self-evident fact. It infuriates them that religionists (or "irrationalists," as Bill Maher calls them) resist what they think is obviously, indisputably true. Believing they know a truth that cannot be known, and that others resist, they are prepared to use any means necessary to silence their opponents and achieve their goals.

3

Radical Faith

IN 1997, THE PSYCHOLOGIST Nicholas Humphrey—a self-styled "liberal"—gave the Amnesty Lecture at Oxford, in which he said that the purpose of his lecture was "to argue in favour of censorship, against freedom of expression." The specific area that he wanted to censor was "moral and religious education . . . especially the education a child receives at home."

> Children have a right not to have their minds addled by nonsense. And we as a society have a duty to protect them from it. So, we should no more allow parents to teach their children to believe, for example, in the literal truth of the Bible . . . than

we should allow parents to knock their children's teeth out
or lock them in a dungeon.[1]

Where have such notions been heard before? Where has
the teaching of the Christian faith been described as child
abuse? In Communist Russia and other totalitarian states.

A Romanian pastor, Richard Wurmbrand, spent four-
teen years imprisoned in Communist Romania, where he
was also tortured. His "crime" was that he publicly declared
Communism and Christianity to be incompatible. In his
book *Tortured for Christ*, Wurmbrand wrote about parents
under Communism who dared to teach their faith to their
children. "If it was discovered that they taught their children
about Christ, their children were taken away from them for
life—with no visitation rights."[2]

Do not mistake this as a parochial issue, affecting only a
persecuted religious community. In America, the war against
Christians is not merely a war against an embattled religion.
It is a war against an imperiled nation—a war against this
nation and its founding principles: the equality of individuals and individual freedom. For these principles are indisputably Christian in origin. They are under siege because they
are insurmountable obstacles to radicals' totalitarian ambition to create a new world in their image.

I know this in my bones because I was born into a family
of political radicals. We were a community of atheist Jews
who described ourselves as "progressives" and identified
our tribe as a persecuted people. The religious holidays we
observed were Chanukah and Passover, whose texts were
drawn from the history of that people and whose lessons, as

we interpreted them, were about freedom from oppression. We purposely did not attend religious services on the High Holy Days—the Days of Awe. These holidays were about individual guilt and repentance. They were about making amends for misdeeds toward one's fellow human beings and settling accounts with the Hebrew God.

In short, the Days of Awe were about the state of individual souls. As progressives and world-changers, we were not interested in the fate of individual souls. Our cause was the salvation of mankind. We wanted justice for oppressed classes and races, and we looked at synagogues as reactionary institutions—houses of superstition whose prayers and preaching served to keep the oppressed in line.

I eventually came to understand that my parents and their friends referred to themselves as "progressives" to hide their true faith, which was Communism. For them, Communism was the vision of a future in which the long history of social injustice would finally come to an end. When I eventually rejected this illusion, I realized that their atheistic creed was itself a form of religious faith. Their God was History, which they viewed as an inexorable march to a promised land.

Like the religionists whom they looked down on, my parents and their leftist friends believed in a redemption, but they thought of *themselves* as the redeemers, not God. The real world into which their faith led them, however, was quite unexpected and the opposite of their utopian vision. A destructive fantasy had seduced them into supporting an empire whose rulers murdered millions.

When Soviet Communism collapsed in 1991, progressives didn't give up their illusions. Instead they changed the name of their utopian dream. Today they no longer call their earthly redemption "Communism." They call it "social justice." Like Communism, social justice is an impossible future in which the inequalities and oppressions that have afflicted human beings for millennia will miraculously vanish and social harmony will rule. The French socialist Auguste Comte called his faith "the religion of humanity," to distinguish it from the religion of God.

What Causes Injustice?

My family and their political comrades prided themselves on the "scientific" basis of their views. They would have been appalled to hear their beliefs described as "religious." But their politics were cut from the same cloth as a famous Christian heresy called Pelagianism. The author of this heresy, Pelagius, was a monk from the British Isles who lived in the fourth century. Although he would not have expressed it this way, Pelagius shared the view of today's progressives—the view that people are naturally good, but society leads them down paths that are bad.

In the language of his faith, Pelagius believed that sins were acts *against* human nature. Therefore, he believed, if enough Christians resisted the temptations of this world and followed the path of righteousness, they could create an earthly paradise—and they could achieve this paradise without help from God. The Pelagian heresy is no different from the progressive notion that if human beings can be made to pursue lives that are politically correct, they can bring about a world of social justice.

Pelagius's view of human benevolence contradicted the church doctrine that sin is an integral part of human nature. The church called this doctrine "original sin," the idea that all human beings share in Adam's sin and are prone to evil, which makes redemption impossible without God. Adam and Eve were born in paradise but forfeited their good fortune because they wanted to know evil. If you eat from the tree of the knowledge of good and evil, the serpent told them, "you shall be as gods." Seduced by this temptation, they defied God's commandment and ate the forbidden fruit.

Their sin was the inevitable result of the free will that was their birthright. Free will gives each individual the power to do good—or evil. Free will makes us the authors of our own choices, our own sins, our own fates—not other people, not classes or races or genders. A corollary of this view is that the potential for evil is present in every individual down through the generations. Because human beings are rebellious and prone to temptation and evil, they will corrupt every effort of redemption. Therefore, there can be no path to an earthly paradise without divine intervention.

The chief proponent of this doctrine was St. Augustine, who condemned Pelagius as a heretic and cast him out of the community of faith. As it happens, the Pelagian heresy was on my mind when I turned my back on the progressive cause.

My exodus was prompted by the murder of a friend of mine, Betty Van Patter. A dedicated, kindhearted leftist and a mother of three children, Betty was the bookkeeper at the New Left magazine *Ramparts*, which I edited. In 1974, I raised the money to buy a Baptist church in East Oakland, California, and turn it into a school for the Black Panther

Party. I also established a nonprofit organization, the Educational Opportunities Corporation, to fund the school, and I recruited Betty to maintain the school's financial ledgers.

Later that year, Betty told a few people she had discovered that the Black Panthers had doctored the books. Some reports have said that she was planning to expose the Panthers' financial improprieties. But Betty believed in her leftist ideology. I think she probably wanted to protect the Panthers, not expose them. But the Panthers viewed her as a white woman who knew too much and couldn't be trusted with their secrets.

On Friday night, December 13, 1974, Betty was at her favorite neighborhood bar, The Berkeley Square, when someone came in and handed her a note. She left with the messenger a short time later and was never seen alive again. Her body was found weeks later in San Francisco Bay. She had been raped and tortured and beaten to death.

I pursued the truth of her murder and discovered that the Black Panther Party was a criminal gang engaging in extortion, arson, drug racketeering, and several murders. The Panthers conducted these crimes while enjoying the support of the leaders and institutions of the American left, including the Democratic Party, local trade unions, and even Oakland business concerns. (The head of Oakland-based Clorox was on the board of directors of the Educational Opportunities Corporation I had created.)

The people who had murdered Betty and engaged in criminal activities were not my political enemies. They were my progressive comrades. The left defended the killers because they were voices of the oppressed and champions of the progressive cause.

Betty had tried to help the Panthers because she believed in that cause. The dream of a liberated future blinded her—as it had blinded me—to the reality of who the Panthers actually were, blinded us to the dangers that killed her. She was just one individual whose life paled into insignificance alongside the cause that mattered to her comrades on the left. So the left's reaction to her murder was . . . silence. That murder—and that silence—shattered my faith in everything I had believed in until then.

The Line Separating Good and Evil

Betty's murder confronted me with a brutal reality: injustice is not caused by an abstraction called "society," as we on the left had maintained. Nor was injustice caused by oppressive races and genders, or solely by our political enemies. Injustice is the result of human selfishness, deceitfulness, malice, envy, greed, and lust. Injustice is the inevitable consequence of our free will as human beings. "Society" is not the cause of injustice. Society is merely a reflection of who we are.

The politically correct, who think it is their mission to save the world, cannot fix the problems that afflict us, because the problems are our creations. Theirs and ours. Because the self-appointed social redeemers seek too much power, and do not understand the source of evil and injustice, they will only make the problems worse—as the romance with Communism has shown.

When I thought about the murder of my friend Betty, even though I was not religious, my first thought was to wish I had understood the doctrine of original sin—the perception that evil runs through the human heart—and through *every* human heart. Whether or not God exists, whether or not the biblical account is true, the doctrine of original sin is an accurate diagnosis of the human condition.

My first encounter with this idea was a passage in *The Gulag Archipelago* by the great Soviet dissident and Christian, Alexander Solzhenitsyn: "The line separating good and evil passes not through states, nor between classes, nor between political parties either, but right through every human heart, and through all human hearts."[3]

In contrast to the progressive mission of saving "society," the goal of Christian belief is saving individual souls. Christians see the imperfections and sufferings of the world as the results of acts by individuals who have failed to do good or have chosen to do evil.

The social redeemers, on the other hand, do not see individuals as agents of their own destinies. They see them as products of "social forces," as objects of class, race, gender, and religious oppressions. Progressives focus on alleged injustices that do not depend on the willful acts of racist or sexist individuals, but on mythical factors like "institutional bias" and "systemic discrimination." Through the progressive lens, individuals and their choices disappear. That is why progressives do not hesitate to impose their solutions on others by force, including the people they propose to save.

These opposing visions are the root cause of the war that is the subject of this book. The social redeemers view the Christian concern for the salvation of individual souls as counterrevolutionary, a *cause* of social oppression. To them, religious believers are obstacles on the path to the future—and must be removed.

That is why progressives have declared war on religious liberty, which is America's founding principle. And that is why they seek to silence and suppress its defenders.

4

Christian America

THE U.S. CAPITOL VISITOR Center opened on December 2, 2008, to serve as a museum and information center for visitors to the nation's capital. The $621 million center is less a monument to the nation's founding and institutions than it is to the antireligious left's vision for America. When it opened, all references to God and faith had been carefully, deliberately edited out of its photos and historical displays.

One panel in particular claimed that the national motto of the United States is *E Pluribus Unum* ("Out of Many, One"). In fact, the national motto, as established by an act of Congress in 1956, is "In God We Trust." A replica of the Speaker's rostrum of the House of Representatives omits the gold-lettered inscription "In God We Trust" above the chair. Photos of the actual Speaker's rostrum were cropped to hide the inscription. A protest by Senator Jim DeMint and other conservative lawmakers led to a rectification of this particular misrepresentation, but many others remained.

The designers of the center had gone to great lengths to alter essential American history. An enlarged image of the Constitution was photoshopped to remove the words "in the Year of our Lord" above the signatures of the signers. The table on which President Lincoln placed his Bible during his second inauguration is on display—just the table, not the Bible.

One of the oddest features of the Capitol Visitor Center is the inscription over the entrance: "We have built no temple but the Capitol. We consult no common oracle but the Constitution."[1]

This is a misquotation of a statement made by an obscure nineteenth-century politician, Rufus Choate, who actually said "We have built no *national* temples but...." Rufus Choate served but one term in the House and one term in the Senate. History remembers Choate as the lawyer who invented the "sleepwalking defense," winning acquittal for a murderer who semidecapitated his mistress while supposedly asleep.

Why did the designers of the Capitol Visitor Center seize on the words of this obscure Whig politician for its welcoming inscription? Apparently, Choate was the only figure in American history who—when misquoted—articulated the leftist vision of an America whose only temple was that of a secular state.[2]

A Secular Republic Built by Christians

In his introduction to *The Portable Atheist*, Christopher Hitchens compares the influence of religionists to a "plague." In the midst of this scurrilous attack, he interrupts himself to say, "I am writing these words on July 4, 2007, the anniversary of the proclamation of the world's first secular republic." The claim that America is "a secular republic" is designed to rebut religionists' contention that America's origins are Christian. But like the argument about the existence of God, the debate over whether America is a Christian nation or secular republic clouds the issue rather than clarifying it.

In fact, both claims are correct. America was indeed the first secular republic, as Hitchens boasts. But America was created as a secular republic *precisely because* of the Christian beliefs of its religious founders—specifically their *Protestant* Christian beliefs.

Beginning with the Pilgrims who landed at Plymouth Rock in 1620, America's founders were mainly members of Protestant sects fleeing persecution by state-sanctioned rival denominations. The Pilgrims signed the famous Mayflower Compact on board the *Mayflower*, which made clear their religious purpose in settling America:

> Having undertaken for the Glory of God, and Advancement of the Christian Faith, and the Honour of our King and Country, a Voyage to plant the first Colony in the northern Parts of Virginia; do by these Presents, solemnly and mutually in the Presence of God and one of another, covenant and combine ourselves together into a civil Body Politick, for our

better Ordering and Preservation, and Furtherance of the Ends aforesaid.

This was the first civil government established by a social contract. The contract embodied the idea that governmental authority derives from the consent of the governed and that all its citizens are entitled to equal treatment under the law. These ideas became the core principles of the future American nation.[3]

The *Mayflower* Pilgrims were fleeing persecution by the Anglican Church, which had become the Church of England in 1534—and thus Britain's official state religion. Anglicans could call on the power of the state to suppress and persecute their religious rivals. Most of the settlers of the American colonies were religious refugees fleeing persecution by a state church. By 1776, 98 percent of the American colonists were Protestants, while Catholics accounted for 1.9 percent and there were 2,500 Jews.[4]

It made no sense to these refugees to create a new nation in the image of the old theocratic states they had fled. To create a new state religion in America would not have even been feasible because they represented a wide array of creeds. As John Adams wrote in a letter to his wife, Abigail, "Because we were so divided in religious sentiments, we could not join in the same act of worship."[5]

In this new nation being formed in the New World, who would have the authority to declare which beliefs were "Christian" and which were not?

America and the Protestant Reformation

Thomas Jefferson, the principal author of the Declaration of Independence and the third president of the United States (from 1801 to 1809), was well aware of the destructive nature of religious disputes. In November 1816, Jefferson wrote a letter to his friend Mathew Carey, a Philadelphia publisher. Carey had asked Jefferson if he planned to publish his views on religion. Jefferson replied that he would write nothing for publication on the subject of religion.

"On the *dogmas* of religion," Jefferson explained, "as distinguished from moral principles, all mankind from the beginning of the world to this day have been quarreling, fighting, burning and torturing one another, for abstractions unintelligible to themselves and to all others, and absolutely beyond the comprehension of the human mind."[6]

The founders of the new nation represented many different religious ideas and traditions, including differing views of what "true Christianity" should be. They were committed to the Protestant ideal of freedom of conscience and religious dissent. For these reasons too, it would have been unthinkable to found this new nation as a theocratic government with an official state religion. Creating a secular republic, then, was a necessary condition for their religious freedom.

For 150 years prior to the Declaration of Independence, the colonies experimented with various forms of government. Some settlements, like Rhode Island and Pennsylvania, chose to be ecumenical and tolerant. Others, like Plymouth and the Massachusetts Bay Colony, chose to be theocratic and intolerant. Six of the thirteen colonies established official religions and imposed criminal punishments on those who deviated from religious decrees. These criminal punishments sometimes included the death penalty. A notorious case was the Salem witch trials.

By 1776, the colonists had come to a revolutionary conclusion. These experiments in colonial government had persuaded them that theocratic government was not only a bad idea, but an un-Christian idea as well. A theocracy was invariably oppressive because it allowed no room for dissent, no freedom of conscience for the individual. Contrary to the claims of Christopher Hitchens and other detractors of Christianity, America is the logical, if not inevitable, development of the Protestant Reformation.

"Endowed by Their Creator . . ."

Two core doctrines of the Protestant Reformation were "justification by faith" and "the priesthood of all believers." The first reflected the Augustinian view that human beings are flawed and sinful by nature and, therefore, can only be saved by God's grace. This led logically to the American idea that government requires a system of checks and balances to restrain the devious impulses and desires of its citizens and officials. As James Madison, one of the principal framers of the Constitution, put it: "If men were angels, no government would be necessary."[7]

The second doctrine, "the priesthood of all believers," was a rejection of the idea that an individual's relation to God had to be mediated through an institution, specifically the Catholic Church. This doctrine freed individuals to define their own conceptions of God and stripped all churches of the authority to facilitate or thwart the saving of their souls. "The priesthood of all believers" leveled the spiritual playing field, making all Christians—and all God's children—equal in the eyes of their Creator.

Thanks to the religious convictions of the American founders, these revolutionary ideas from the Protestant Reformation had an impact far beyond the confines of Protestant churches. The concept of "the priesthood of all believers" led directly to the principle at the heart of the Declaration of Independence, that "all men are created equal" and endowed with rights by their Creator—rights no government has the authority to deny.

The fact that neither the Declaration of Independence nor the Constitution employs Christian language is a logical result of the Protestant view that Christians are free to disagree about what it means to be Christian. Among the American founders, there was great latitude on this point. For example, Thomas Jefferson was practically a religious denomination unto himself. He famously edited the New Testament, eliminating all references to Jesus's divinity.

Benjamin Franklin was also uncertain of the divinity of Jesus. He summarized his typically American mixture of skepticism, tolerance, and belief in a letter to Ezra Stiles, a Congregationalist minister and then-president of Yale College. In that letter, written a month before his death, Franklin summarized his minimalist convictions: "I believe in one God, creator of the universe. That he governs it by his Providence. That he ought to be worshipped. That the most acceptable service we render to him is doing good to his other children."[8]

The Declaration's proclamation that all men are created equal and endowed by their Creator with unalienable rights was unique in the history of nations. It led to the abolition of slavery and the enfranchisement of women. Members of Hitchens's godless faith could not have created this American framework, because it is only the fact that the basic rights to life, liberty, and the pursuit of happiness are seen as gifts from God that they are unalienable. Government did not give them, and therefore government cannot take them away. Without the founders' belief in God—fiction or not—America could not exist.

The Most Important Right

The first and most important right guaranteed in the Bill of Rights is religious liberty, along with its related rights to free assembly, a free press, and freedom of speech. Long ago, the philosopher Aristotle declared courage to be the most important of the virtues, because without courage one could not defend and sustain the other virtues. The right to religious liberty and its ancillary right to free speech occupy a similar place among political virtues. If individuals do not have freedom of conscience, if they are not free to articulate and defend what they believe, they will not be able to defend any of their freedoms.

Consequently, the framers of the Bill of Rights made the guarantee of these rights its very first order of business: "Congress shall make no law respecting an establishment of religion, nor prohibiting the free exercise thereof."[9] The first of the two clauses in this sentence forbids the formation of a state religion; the second guarantees all Americans the free-dom to express and exercise their religious beliefs. It is the "Free Exercise Clause" that has become the first casualty of the war against religion, and America.

5

Prayer in the Schools

IN THE CAFETERIA OF Carillon Elementary School in Oviedo, Florida, a five-year-old girl bowed her head to say grace before eating lunch. Moments later, a school employee, a lunchroom monitor, bent down beside the child and told her it was wrong to pray at school, and she must never do so again.[1]

A Memphis, Tennessee, elementary school teacher gave a writing assignment to her class, telling her students to write about their heroes and explain why they looked up to them. Ten-year-old Erin Shead chose to write about God. When Erin turned in her assignment, the teacher refused to accept it. In fact, the teacher said, Erin had to take her paper off school property immediately because just having it in the classroom where her classmates might see it could violate the First Amendment. Some students overheard the teacher rebuking Erin and later mocked her for believing in God. After school, Erin asked her mother why it was wrong to talk about God in school.[2]

At Helen Hunt-Jackson Elementary School in Temecula, California, a teacher assigned a class of first graders to give a one-minute "show-and-tell" presentation about family holiday traditions. One girl, Brynn Williams, held up a star of Bethlehem ornament from the family Christmas tree, briefly told the class about the birth of Jesus, then began to recite a Bible verse. The teacher interrupted her and told her, "Go take your seat." Brynn was the only student prevented from finishing her talk. Brynn's father later said that she was hurt and humiliated, feared she was going to be punished, and couldn't understand what she had done wrong.[3]

These are just a few examples of how religious ideas have been banned in American schools. Hundreds of similar incidents have been reported by the news media. The framers of the Constitution wrote the First Amendment to *prevent* the suppression of religious freedom that is now epidemic in American schools. The First Amendment *expressly* guarantees a child's right to voluntarily pray, and to write about and speak about his or her religious beliefs, openly and freely in front of other students. Yet teachers, administrators, and even school cafeteria workers now regard it as their responsibility to police small children to prevent them from expressing their religious beliefs. This can all be traced to a disastrous Supreme Court decision rendered nearly six decades ago.

A Wall of Separation

In 1962, a landmark case about religious liberty, known as *Engel v. Vitale*, came before the U.S. Supreme Court. It was the forerunner of a series of cases that would ban any discussion of God from public schools and bar religion from the public square.

The suit was brought by a group of five liberals—three Jews and two self-described "spiritual" people. They complained that a brief voluntary prayer written by the New York Board of Regents, addressed to "Almighty God," violated their "religious beliefs" (even though some of them were atheists). The Regents' prayer was to be read every day at the opening of school. This is the full 23-word text of the prayer: "Almighty God, we acknowledge our dependence upon Thee, and we beg Thy blessings upon us, our parents, our teachers and our country. Amen."

Steven Engel and his fellow plaintiffs were represented by the radical American Civil Liberties Union. Engel himself was a founding member of the ACLU's New York affiliate. Before taking the case to the highest court in the nation, the group had lost before three state courts. The majority opinion of the New York Supreme Court was particularly contemptuous of their constitutional claim:

Not only is this prayer not a violation of the First Amendment (no decision of this or of the United States Supreme Court says or suggests that it is) but a holding that it is such a violation would be in defiance of all American history, and such a holding would destroy a part of the essential foundation of the American governmental structure. . . . That the First Amendment was ever intended to forbid as an "establishment of religion" a simple declaration of belief in God is so contrary to history as to be impossible of acceptance.[4]

Engel and the ACLU were not discouraged by their defeats. They took their suit to the nation's highest court where, by a six to one majority, the justices rejected the three lower court judgments. The Court ruled that the Board of Regents' prayer was a violation of the Constitution's Establishment Clause. Speaking for the majority, which included four prominent liberals, Justice Hugo Black rejected the defense's two key arguments: (1) that the prayer was voluntary and (2) that it reflected no particular religion. The Court majority held that, because the prayer did not address the belief of atheists, it violated the Establishment Clause.

Justice Black did not cite a single legal precedent or court decision in his majority opinion—because there were none. As the religious website Free2Pray.info observed: "For 170 years following the ratification of the *Constitution* and *Bill of Rights*, no Court had ever struck down any prayer, in any form, in any location."[5]

Many years after the 1962 decision, the plaintiff, Steven Engel, was interviewed about his thoughts on the case. Engel characterized (or mischaracterized) the views of people on the other side of the case this way:

You can disguise it anyway you want—and there seem to be new disguises every day in this area, such as school vouchers—but it all comes down to the same thing. There are many who would love to stick their hand in the public till because they feel imposed upon and feel they are taxed unjustly for public education that they don't participate in. I understand that, but I still pay for a lot of things that I think are unjust like the Vietnam War and the war in Iraq.[6]

Engel viewed the question of prayer in schools as a quarrel over taxation and ideology. He saw his opponents as a political faction that was disgruntled over having to pay to support an educational system which censored their political views. Engel was simply oblivious to the central role that religious beliefs have played in shaping American government and American freedoms, including the freedom to dissent.

The legal argument the ACLU used to support Engel and his fellow plaintiffs was that the Regents' nondenominational prayer violated the Establishment Clause. The ACLU backed its argument not with a clause in the Constitution, but with a phrase taken from a private letter written by President Thomas Jefferson. In a letter to the Danbury Baptist Association of Connecticut on January 1, 1802, Jefferson wrote that the First Amendment, enacted on behalf of all the American people, "declared that their legislature should 'make no law respecting an establishment of religion, or prohibiting the free exercise thereof,' thus building a wall of separation between Church & State."[7]

Jefferson coined the metaphor of a wall of church-state separation to assure the Baptists in Connecticut that the government would never infringe on the free exercise of their religion. The ACLU stood Jefferson's reassurance on its head, turning it into a rationale for *suppressing* the free exercise of religion. That phrase, "wall of separation between church and state," became a bumper-sticker slogan for leftists and secularists who want to silence religious people and marginalize their beliefs.

We don't have to guess at Jefferson's actual thoughts on the issue, because he himself invoked God and nonsectarian religious beliefs in the documents he drafted. The most famous example is the Declaration of Independence, which states that God the Creator is the source of our "unalienable rights." Jefferson also drafted the Virginia Statute for Religious Freedom, which begins, "Whereas, Almighty God hath created the mind free . . . ."

Clearly, Jefferson did not see a nonsectarian invoking of God as an "establishment of religion." The lone dissenter on the court bench, Justice Potter Stewart noted that under the First Amendment government endorsements of religion had been common in America since its inception in phrases such as "God save the United States and this Honorable Court," and didn't think that allowing schoolchildren to pray in a nondenominational manner served to establish a religion: "We deal here not with the establishment of a state church, which would, of course, be constitutionally impermissible, but with whether school children who want to begin their day by joining in prayer must be prohibited from doing so."

Changing the Culture by Force

To grasp the full implications of the Court's decision, consider the process by which school prayer was outlawed. Prayer had been a common practice in public schools across the country for nearly two centuries and had never been seen as an establishment of religion. Reasonable people can differ over the practice of prayer in a public institution. There are many democratic platforms available for resolving disagreements that don't involve a blanket ban on school prayer from the Supreme Court bench. Most religious people would agree to making an accommodation for children from a minority viewpoint (such as atheism) so they wouldn't feel excluded.

If the plaintiffs in *Engel v. Vitale* were primarily interested in protecting their children from being offended by the Regents' prayer, they could have sought to remedy their concerns at the local or state level. They could have organized other parents to press for a change in how the prayer was implemented. Since the Regents are elected by the state legislature, Engel and the other plaintiffs could have lobbied their representatives to seek an ecumenical solution that would have been acceptable to all. Instead they bypassed the democratic channels and pursued a constitutional challenge in the courts. They did so because victory in this arena would make their partisan view the new fundamental law of the land.

Engel and his fellow plaintiffs lost the case three times in three lower courts: the Supreme Court of New York (1959), the Appellate Division of the Supreme Court of New York (1960), and the Court of Appeals of New York (1961). None of these lower courts agreed with the plaintiffs' claim that the 23-word Regents' prayer constituted the establishment of a state religion. Undeterred, and empowered by the financial and legal support of the ACLU, the plaintiffs took their case to the Supreme Court. They hoped to obtain the result they wanted through a handful of black-robed, politically appointed lawyers in Washington, whose lifetime tenures insulated them from the consequences of their decisions.

This was clearly not the best or most American way to resolve a complex dispute with such wide-ranging ramifications. If it was in the best interest of the nation to overturn 170 years of a tradition established by the founders themselves, shouldn't it have taken place through the democratic process rather than an autocratic judicial decree by a handful of individuals?

A small group of atheists had found a sympathetic ear among six unelected justices, and changed not only the policy of a school system, but the fundamental law of the land. In the process, they created a "constitutional right" that had never existed before—the right of a nonbelieving minority to deny the majority of Americans *their* right to express their belief in God while at school. This decision set forces in motion that would change the culture and alter the course of a nation.

Engel v. Vitale became the basis for other decisions that continued the attack. In *Wallace v. Jaffree* (1985), the Supreme Court ruled that an Alabama law permitting one minute for "for meditation or voluntary prayer" was unconstitutional. The decision defies reason, since even an atheist could not object to "meditation," meaning contemplation or reflection. In *Lee v. Weisman* (1992), the Supreme Court banned clergy-led prayer at middle school commencement ceremonies. In 2000, the Supreme Court used the precedent of *Lee v. Weisman* as a basis for *Santa Fe ISD v. Doe*, a decision that expanded the ban to include school-organized *student-led* prayer at high school football games.[8]

In one despotic decision after another, the Supreme Court inflated the Establishment Clause while letting all the air out of the Free Exercise protection. Again and again, the High Court jammed its radical redefinition of the First Amendment down the throat of an unwilling, unready society.

America came under the grip of a bizarre official hypocrisy: Both houses of Congress opened with prayer. The Supreme Court opened with the invocation, "God save the United States and this Honorable Court." The lunch money that jingled in the pockets of schoolchildren was stamped "In God We Trust"—but "God" could not be invoked in any public school in America.

A Wall of Separation between Classmates

The extent to which the anti-prayer forces were willing to go to cleanse religious expression from public schools was vividly demonstrated in the case of Kayla Broadus, a kindergartener in Saratoga Springs, New York. She had the temerity during snack time to take the hands of two classmates, bow her head, and pray, "God is good. God is great. Thank you, God, for my food." Her horrified teacher rushed over to scold and silence her.

The teacher reported Kayla's crime to the school attorney, who declared it a violation of the "separation of church and state." The school principal sent Kayla's parents a letter saying, "Please be advised that Kayla will not be permitted to ask other students to join her in prayer prior to snacktime or lunchtime."

Kayla's mother responded by filing suit and obtaining a temporary restraining order. The case was settled without trial. Under the settlement, the school district acknowledged Kayla's right to pray out loud, so long as she did not disturb her classmates—or invite them to pray with her.[9] Unfortunately, the settlement also preserved the so-called "wall of separation between church and state"—and between Kayla and her friends. A five-year-old may not invite her classmates to join in thanking God for their food.

What kind of America is this? Whatever happened to "the land of the free"? Where is the principle of tolerance and respect, which is the indispensable foundation of American pluralism?

The "Ministry of Truth"

Winston Smith, the protagonist of George Orwell's *Nineteen Eighty-Four*, works at the Ministry of Truth. His job is to falsify history to fit the party line. If Big Brother made a prediction last year that turned out to be wrong, Winston Smith would alter the past to make it agree with present reality. This way, Big Brother would never be wrong.

Engel v. Vitale practically required that the American public education system establish its own Orwellian Ministry of Truth. Once the left had built a wall of separation between church and state, it had to change history and make the past conform to the present. The schools could not describe the religious origins of American freedoms without violating

Engel v. Vitale. For this reason, the Pilgrims had to be deleted from our children's textbooks. Thus, in 2002, the New Jersey Department of Education removed references to the Pilgrims and the Mayflower from its history standards for school textbooks. Other states that do not require any mention of the Pilgrims in history textbooks include Virginia and Indiana. The problem? "The word Pilgrim implies religion," said Brian Jones of the Education Leaders Council, adding, "It's getting more difficult to talk about the Bible and the Puritans." Some school systems blur historical truth by referring to the Pilgrims as "early settlers," "newcomers," or "European colonizers."[10]

In 1986, twenty-four years after *Engel v. Vitale*, NYU professor Paul Vitz published a study of censorship and bias in public school textbooks. Vitz examined sixty social studies textbooks used by 87 percent of public school students. Among his conclusions:

> It is common in these books to treat Thanksgiving without explaining to whom the Pilgrims gave thanks. . . . The Pilgrims are described entirely without any reference to religion; thus at the end of their first year they "wanted to give thanks for all they had" . . . so they had the first Thanksgiving. But no mention is made of the fact that it was God they were thanking. . . .
>
> The Pueblo [Indians] can pray to Mother Earth—but Pilgrims can't be described as praying to God. And never are Christians described as praying to Jesus, either in the United States or elsewhere, in the present or even in the past. . . . There is not one story or article in all these books, in approximately

nine to ten thousand pages, in which the central motivation or major content derives from Christianity or Judaism.[11]

Censorship and the rewriting of history are the practices of totalitarian regimes. In a perverse way, the current anti-religious bias of liberal justices and textbook publishers shows how the absence of religion from our historical memory not only distorts our history, but undermines our present liberties. As our freedoms are steadily diminished under the onslaught of "political correctness" and social justice fanatics, the *true* story of American freedom must be revised, rewritten, and censored by school officials, textbook publishers, and other tentacles of our "Ministry of Truth."

No Separation of Mosque and State?

Since the real animus behind the assault on religious freedom is an assault on the America that religious refugees created, it is not surprising to find a grim hypocrisy at its core. Following the 9/11 Islamist terrorist attacks, religious proselytizing was permitted and even encouraged in American schools. The American Civil Liberties Union didn't protest. The Freedom from Religion Foundation didn't object. The left had purged all Christian references and prayers from the public schools, but this new wave of proselytizing was perfectly acceptable to them because it was proselytizing on behalf of Islam, whose jihadist elements had declared war on the West. Leftists don't object to religion being taught in schools, apparently, so long as the religion is opposed to Western values in general, and American values in particular.

In January 2018, Libby Hilsenrath and Nancy Gayer, two mothers of students at Chatham Middle School in New Jersey, filed a federal lawsuit against the school. Their complaint: the school had shown two videos to their students' classes that were clearly designed to convert viewers to Islam. One was called *Intro to Islam*. The video included such statements as:

Allah is the one God who created the heavens and the earth, who has no equal and is all powerful.

What is the Noble Quran? Divine Revelation sent to Muhammad, last Prophet of Allah. A Perfect guide for Humanity.

May God help us all find the true faith, Islam.

The other video, *5 Pillars*, presented the tenets of Islam in a computer-animated cartoon in which a Muslim boy, Yusuf, explains his religion to his non-Muslim friend, Alex. At the end of the video, Alex is sad that he is not going with Yusuf to pray. Then Yusuf invites Alex to "come see how I pray," and the boys go off happily together.[12]

Represented by the Thomas More Law Center, Hilsenrath and Gayer filed their lawsuit as a last resort. They had first appealed directly to the school board to remove the videos from the lesson plan but were rebuffed. When they continued to pursue a resolution of their complaints, the mothers were attacked on social media as "bigots" and "Islamophobes" and called "hateful," "ignorant," "intolerant," and "racist." The federal suit filed by the Thomas More Law Center noted that the lessons presented Islam as a "religious fact" and gave a "sugarcoated, false depiction of Islam." Students "were not informed of the kidnappings, beheadings, slave-trading, massacres, and persecution of non-Muslims, nor the repression of women—all done in the name of Islam."[13]

Far from being unique, this attempted indoctrination reflected a practice widespread in American schools after 9/11. In 2015, students at Spring Hill Middle School in Tennessee were required to write, "There is no god but Allah; Muhammad is his prophet."[14] Students at Mountain Ridge Middle School in Gerrardstown, West Virginia, were forced to write the same Islamic profession of faith under the guise of performing a "calligraphy exercise."[15]

In 2003 students in the Byron Union School District in California were given an exercise in which they were told, "From the beginning, you and your classmates will become Muslims."[16] Students were made to memorize portions of the first chapter of the Quran and the Islamic profession of faith, to adopt Muslim names, and to shout "Allahu akbar." They were even encouraged to skip lunch to simulate the Ramadan fast. "By way of contrast," observed Paul E. Sperry, a media fellow at the Hoover Institution, "a companion unit on Christianity did not require students to pretend they were any kind of Christian, recite any Scripture, or memorize any Christian prayer."[17]

The Thomas More Law Center represented parents who complained about the Byron school exercise. The More Law Center's chief counsel observed:

While public schools prohibit Christian students from reading the Bible, praying, displaying the Ten Commandments, and even mentioning the word "God," students in California are being indoctrinated into the religion of Islam. Public schools would never tolerate teaching Christianity in this way. Just imagine the ACLU's outcry if students were told that they had to pray the Lord's Prayer, memorize the Ten Commandments, use such phrases as 'Jesus is the Messiah,' and fast during Lent.[18]

The double standard exposed the left's agenda of purging Judeo-Christian values and history from the public schools. If those on the left were genuinely concerned about the integrity of the First Amendment (as they interpret it), the same alleged "wall" that separates church and state would also separate mosque and state. Instead, the left celebrates not just teaching about Islam but actively *proselytizing* for Islam in the public schools.

Why? It's because Christian doctrines were foundational to the American Republic, which the left despises. Fundamentalist Islam has declared war on "infidel" cultures like America's, with its Judeo-Christian respect for individual liberty and constitutional restraints on the power of government. On their hatred of Christianity and contempt for the Constitution, both the left and political Islam agree.[19]

6

The War Begins

THE **1960**S SAW THE emergence of a world-class provoca-
teur and media celebrity, Madalyn Murray, the founder
and president of American Atheists. She filed a lawsuit which
could be called the Fort Sumter of the war over religious liberty. Like the South Carolina fort where the first shots of the
Civil War were fired, the lawsuit known as *Murray v. Curlett*
ignited a cultural civil war in America by vaulting Murray to
national prominence. She would continue to be the symbol
of American atheism until her murder in 1995 at the hands
of one of her followers.

In 1960, prior to the *Engel v. Vitale* ruling, Murray filed a suit
against the Baltimore City Public School System, claiming
it was unconstitutional for the public schools to require her

fourteen-year-old son William to participate in Bible readings (specifically the daily recital of the Lord's Prayer). Judge J. Gilbert Pendergast of the Baltimore City court dismissed the petition stating, "It is abundantly clear that petitioner's real objective is to drive every concept of religion out of the public school system." This was certainly Murray's objective and also that of the American Civil Liberties Union, which provided her with financial support and legal expertise.

Her lawsuit, *Murray v. Curlett*, reached the United States Supreme Court in 1963, combined with a similar case from Pennsylvania, *Abington School District v. Schempp*. One year after striking down school prayer in *Engel v. Vitale*, the Court voted eight to one in Madalyn Murray's favor, banning mandatory reading or recitation of the Bible at public schools. Once again, Justice Potter Stewart was the lone dissenter.

The Most Hated Woman in America

After 170 years in which prayers were said and the Bible was read daily in schools across the nation, the practice was declared unconstitutional overnight. So much for *stare decisis*. The Court majority defended its ruling on the grounds that the Establishment Clause required the state to be neutral toward religion. Justice Stewart argued that the decision led "not to true neutrality with respect to religion, but to the establishment of a religion of secularism." The *Wall Street Journal* agreed, saying that atheism was now "the one belief to which the state's power will extend its *protection*."[1]

Once again, an issue that could have been addressed in local deliberative bodies was elevated to the constitutional level. Instead of working with school district officials to reach an accommodation, or democratically electing school board members through local elections, Murray took her complaint to the Supreme Court, where nine political appointees voted to change the fundamental law of the land and alienate its religious citizens.

Murray had already gained notoriety through her battles with the Baltimore school district. After her Supreme Court victory, *Life* magazine wrote a cover story, crowning her "The Most Hated Woman in America." Hated or not, the *New York Times* treated her Supreme Court victory as an epic achievement in blaring front-page headlines, accompanied by favorable stories spread across three pages. *The Today Show* celebrated her birthday on its feature segment, "Great People Born Today."[2]

Murray took a perverse pride in being named "The Most Hated Woman in America." She learned early on that provoking the public to anger always generated publicity—and gained her sympathy and support from the leftists and liberals who dominated the culture. She even used her sons' pets to tweak the American public. After her boys were harassed by the neighborhood children because of her activities, she bought two dogs to protect them. She told her son William, "Let's give them names that will infuriate everyone." She named them Marx and Engels.[3]

Murray savored the death threats and curses she received, wrote them down, and published them. She even saved a hate letter smeared with feces and showed it to horrified reporters, who then promoted her cause.[4] Like the New Left radicals who supported her, she provoked her opponents with foul language and outrageous acts, once tearing up a Bible on the

Phil Donahue Show in front of millions of television viewers.[5] Never did anyone love being hated more.

Clauses in Collision

For nearly 200 years, the two religion clauses in the First Amendment had been plainly understood by the Congress, the Supreme Court, and the American people: First, Congress could not establish an official state religion. Second, Congress could not prohibit the free exercise of religion. In all that time, there had never been any tension between the Establishment Clause and the Free Exercise Clause, because both clauses worked together to ensure maximum freedom of religion for all Americans.

Suddenly, in two decisions in 1962 and 1963, the Establishment Clause was radically reinterpreted—and the two religion clauses of the First Amendment collided head-on. In order for the Establishment Clause to mean what the Supreme Court now said it meant—that all prayer, all Bible reading and recitation, all reference to God was strictly forbidden in public schools—the free exercise of religion had to give way. The radically reinterpreted Establishment Clause became a hungry piranha in the goldfish bowl of First Amendment rights, eating up all the others. Not only is it now unconstitutional to freely exercise religion in a public school, but the freedom of speech is abridged (prayer is speech). Freedom of the press is shut down (God has been edited out of our history textbooks). The right of the people to peaceably assemble on school grounds (such as a prayer huddle after a game or a baccalaureate service) is severely restricted.

The Supreme Court imposed an extreme minority point of view onto the nation's founding framework, declaring nearly two centuries of prayer in American schools unconstitutional. To reverse two centuries of well-accepted practice and tradition with such a sweeping and arbitrary decision was bound to be divisive and give rise to resistance among religious people.

More than thirty years after the decision, Robert J. McKeever of London's Institute of the Americas published an analysis of the impact of Supreme Court decisions on American society. He concluded:

> The Court's school prayer decisions were, and still are, deeply unpopular with the public, many politicians and most religious organizations. Indeed, in a country where 95 percent of the population believe in God and some 60 percent belong to a religious organization, it comes as no surprise to learn that in a 1991 opinion poll, 78 percent of Americans support the reintroduction of school prayer.[6]

Playing the Victim

How did Murray gain the sympathy of enough Americans to prevail in her cause? By playing the victim and capitalizing on Americans' respect for maverick actors. Counterculture publisher Paul Krassner recruited Murray to write a column for *The Realist*, a "guerilla" publication of the New Left movement. In her maiden column, she delivered a cornucopia of taunts: "Some people have interpreted my position to mean that I am against religious ceremonies in schools. This is not true. I am against religion. I am against schools. I am against apple pies. I am against 'Americanism.' . . . I'm even against giving the country back to the Indians. Why should the poor fools be stuck with this mess?"[7] The sixties counterculture loved this. When others reacted with anger—and they inevitably did—she knew she had won.

Murray portrayed herself, her son William, and atheists in general as underdogs—victims of a bigoted and hateful Christian majority. Playing the victim was the surest way to win the sympathies of liberal Americans, even liberals who considered her too extreme. She wrote a lengthy letter to the *Baltimore Sun*, and though she was an anti-Semite herself, quoted Shakespeare's persecuted Jew, Shylock, from *The Merchant of Venice*, substituting "atheist" for "Jew": "Hath not an Atheist eyes? Hath not an Atheist hands, organs, dimensions, senses, affections, passions? Fed with the same food, hurt with the same weapons, subject to the same diseases, healed by the same means, warmed and cooled by the same winter and summer as a Christian is?"[8]

Intrigued by Murray's "Shylock" letter to the newspaper, and a ten-day "strike" she had announced, to keep her son home from school in protest, a reporter from the *Baltimore Sun* showed up at the Murrays' door to interview them. The reporter wrote a lengthy and sympathetic article headlined, "Boy of 14 Balks at Prayer in School." The article ignited nationwide media interest, including TV and radio shows. Murray claimed that more than a hundred articles on her protest appeared over the next few weeks in the three Baltimore papers.[9]

The role of professional victim came naturally to Murray, who lived with her parents and whose family life was a permanent battlefield, with her father—"Pup"—her chief enemy. Her son William's memoir describes scenes of horrifying violence between them. The book opens with a dinner table scene that William witnessed as an eight-year-old—an argument between Murray and Pup that turned violent. Murray and Pup had quarreled over her radical politics, and Pup had criticized her disorderly life and "loose morals" (a recurring theme in their fights). He berated her for having two sons out of wedlock and failing to take care of them, leaving Murray's mother to bring them up.

At one point, while hurling plates at her father and her brother, who was also present, Murray threatened, "I'll kill you!" Since she was brandishing a ten-inch butcher knife, the threat seemed real. Pup and her brother rushed her and were able to disarm her. After the struggle, young William saw that both men had been slashed and bloodied. There was blood dotting the walls. Murray shrieked at her father, "I'll see you dead. I'll get you yet. I'll walk on your grave!" Then she ran out of the room.[10]

William Murray recalled his home life this way: "Mine was not the typical American family, where a dad and a mom and the kids cuddled up on the couch with hot chocolate and popcorn to watch *Father Knows Best*. At my house, we argued about the value of the American Way, whether or not the workers should revolt, and why the Pope, Christians and Jews—anybody who believed in God—were morons."[11]

America—a "Fascist Slave Labor Camp"
During the 1950s, Murray joined the Socialist Labor Party and then the Socialist Workers Party, immersing herself ever

more deeply in radical politics. She met with Communist Party leaders and moved so far left that, in the spring and summer of 1960, she set out with her two sons to go to Europe, intending to renounce her American citizenship and defect to the Soviet Union. She made repeated attempts to defect through the Soviet embassies in Paris and Rome, but the Soviets rebuffed her each time. They may have been wary of granting political asylum to an obviously disturbed individual.

Finally, in September 1960, Murray returned to the States with her two boys. She enrolled William at Woodbourne Junior High, part of Baltimore's public school system (he had previously attended private schools). As she walked with William down a school corridor, they passed classrooms where students recited the Pledge of Allegiance and the Lord's Prayer. Hearing the prayer, she became visibly angry. She took William to the office and confronted the principal about the prayers she heard coming from the classrooms.

The principal told her that if she didn't like these practices and traditions, she was free to enroll William in a private school—or, he added, she could sue the Baltimore Board of Education. It was a fateful suggestion. Murray went home and began preparing the campaign that would take her to the Supreme Court and national notoriety.

As they returned home, Murray questioned William about his experiences at school, something she'd never done before. He told her he had taken part in school prayers and Bible readings for years—it didn't bother him. When he told her that, William recalled, "She cursed me roundly, accusing me of being stupid and brainless, like all men."

Then she gave him instructions: "Tomorrow morning I want you to start keeping a log of what happens during the school day. Make special notes on any activities that smack of religion in any form: prayers, Bible readings, songs. You know why, don't you?"

"No, Mom, I don't, really. The guy said the majority wants—"[12]

Murray slapped her son hard and said, "You stupid fool." She continued:

> Don't you understand what is going on yet?... The United States is nothing more than a fascist slave labor camp run by a handful of Jew bankers in New York City. They trick you into believing you're free with those phony rigged elections. ... The only way true freedom can be achieved is through the new socialist man. We have to achieve an entire race that lives for the state. ... Russia is close but not close enough or they would have let us in.... Well, if they'll keep us from going to Russia, where there is some freedom, we'll just have to change America.[13]

That's how Murray's lawsuit began. But that's not how it was presented to the public—or the court.

A Ruthless Strategy: Blame the Christians

During the next two years, right up to the Supreme Court decision, she played the victim role skillfully and relentlessly. She created a false narrative, which is aptly summarized on the back cover of *An Atheist Epic*—the book she wrote about her anti-God crusade:

An Atheist Epic tells the dramatic story of how fourteen-year-old William J. Murray III and his mother Madalyn Murray (later O'Hair) challenged the compulsory recitation of the Lord's Prayer and forced reading of the Christian Bible in the public schools of Baltimore. It tells of the beatings young Bill received with the approval of school authorities, police, and courts, and of the attacks on the Murray home instigated and led by good Christians—attacks that led quite directly to the fatal heart attack suffered by Mrs. Murray's father. It describes the Christian execution of little Garth's kitten and the sorry demise of the two "Atheist dogs" that Bill and Garth had as companions after loss of the kitten. Virtually all the religious attacks upon the First Amendment–mandated separation of state and church that America has endured since 1963 have been in retaliation to *Murray v. Curlett*—the case that Madalyn successfully took all the way to the U.S. Supreme Court to obtain the ruling that forced prayer and Bible reading were unconstitutional.

According to William, *An Atheist Epic* by Madalyn Murray O'Hair (she added "O'Hair" after marrying Richard O'Hair in 1965) was a highly spun and unreliable version of events. The back-cover blurb was even less honest than the book itself. In the book, Murray doesn't claim to know who killed the cat, but the blurb blames a "Christian execution" for the pet's death.

One false claim in particular sheds a glaring light on Murray's character and her ruthless strategy—her claim that Christians were responsible for her father's death.

One morning in January 1963, six months before the Supreme Court rendered its decision, Madalyn and her father were at the breakfast table, arguing bitterly. Finally, she stood and headed for the door, shouting at her father, "I hope you drop dead. I'll dump your shriveled body in the trash!" William, who was sixteen at the time, recalled, "She slammed the door and was gone. Grandfather sat down, his hands shaking as he lifted his cup of coffee to his lips."[14]

That afternoon her father went to the supermarket. While talking to a friend at the checkout stand, he clutched his chest and fell over dead. Later that day, Murray returned home, ready to resume the fight. She called out to her mother, "Where's the old man?" and let a few epithets fly.

Her mother walked into the room, looked her daughter in the eye, and said: "You got your wish. You wished your father dead this morning, and dead he is. He had a heart attack at the A&P."

According to William, his mother said, "Well, I'll be. Where's the stiff?" She then told William to make some calls, find the lowest-priced undertaker, and order "a cheap wood box."[15]

When the family gathered at the mortuary, Murray had second thoughts. She changed her orders and demanded the most expensive casket the funeral home offered. Was it remorse that changed her mind—or a political calculation? The Supreme Court decision was only months away. A situation had presented itself that she could manipulate to her advantage. She took the receipt for the funeral expenses (the receipt was prominently marked "paid") and placed it next to Pup's body. Then she maintained a vigil at the casket for two days.[16]

In an interview with *Playboy*, she told the story of Pup's death this way: "Late one night our house was attacked with stones and bricks by five or six young Christians, and my father got very upset and frightened. Well, the next day he dropped dead of a heart attack."[17] Years later she dedicated her book, *An Atheist Epic*, to her father with these lines:

> This book is for
>
> Pup
>
> who died in Baltimore Md.,
>
> . . . and for
>
> those glorious Christians,
>
> known to us by name,
>
> who killed him.

How did the First Amendment guarantee of religious freedom change overnight into a suppression of that same freedom? A circus put on by a calculating, truth-challenged, anti-American crackpot, egged on by ACLU radicals, provided an opportunity for eight lifetime political appointees, elected by no one and accountable to no one, to reinterpret the Constitution, overturn nearly two centuries of precedent and tradition, and change the life of a nation.

7

Moving the World

IN THE THIRD CENTURY BCE, the Greek scientist Archimedes stood before King Hiero II of Syracuse, explaining the physics of the lever to the king. "Give me a lever," he said, "and a place to stand, and I will move the earth."

With the Supreme Court's prayer decision, the social redeemers had found their lever. They had bypassed America's democratic platforms, where they were greatly out-numbered, and by a vote of six unelected lawyers, they had overturned nearly two centuries of precedent and tradition. And they had done so for all fifty states—at once.

People like Steven Engel and Madalyn Murray and groups like the ACLU represented a minority in America. But the Court's power to reinterpret the Constitution was so broad, and its authority so absolute, that this radical minority was able to impose its will on *all* Americans. The Court gave the radicals a lever they could never have attained through the democratic process. With that lever, they moved the nation and advanced their dream of a liberated future in a way they could not have previously imagined.

The war against prayer in schools had coincided with the rise of a radical movement, which referred to itself as a "New Left," and bore a hostility toward America that only "Old Left" Communists had manifested before. The degree of their revulsion against their country can be measured in the fact that America was then engaged in a life-and-death struggle with a nuclear-armed Communist Russia. Yet the New Left radicals openly declared their opposition to America's anti-Communist cause. To underscore their sympathy for the Communist enemy and hatred for their country, New Left radicals identified themselves as "anti-anti-Communists," and spelled "Amerikkka" with three "k's" to link the entire nation to the Ku Klux Klan.

After winning the fight against school prayer, the radicals widened the war and won victories in two more landmark Supreme Court cases. These were decided on shakier constitutional grounds than the prayer-in-school decisions, sometimes even nonexistent constitutional grounds. The new decisions dramatically altered the government's attitude toward ultimate matters of life and death. Because they circumvented the democratic legislative process, the new Supreme Court decrees may have settled the law, but they didn't change the hearts and minds of the American people. By precluding the formation of a national consensus on these issues, they created political divisions that split the nation more deeply than at any time since the Civil War.

The first of the two cases was *Griswold v. Connecticut* in 1965. The suit challenged an 1879 state law prohibiting the use of "any drug, medicinal article or instrument for the purpose of preventing conception." The plaintiff was Estelle Griswold, executive director of Planned Parenthood. This organization was the offspring of Margaret Sanger, who in 1921 had created its forerunner, the American Birth Control League.

Margaret Sanger, Feminist Radical

Margaret Sanger belonged to a group of leftists who were also associated with the creation of the American Civil Liberties Union. The most prominent figure in this radical circle was Emma Goldman, known as "Red Emma." Goldman was a revolutionary who had plotted with her lover to assassinate Henry Clay Frick, chairman of the Carnegie Steel Company.[1] The plot failed, and she was deported to the Soviet Union.

In her own mind, Sanger, too, was a revolutionary, openly proclaiming that birth control was the means by which she intended to change the world. In March 1914, Sanger launched a monthly newspaper, the *Woman Rebel*, which promoted not only contraception but moral and political anarchy. The paper's motto was "No gods, no masters!" Its pages bristled with such statements as, "The rebel woman claims the right to be an unmarried mother," and asserted that women have a duty to face the world "with a go-to-hell look in the eyes; to have an ideal; to speak and act in defiance of convention."

In a 1930 profile of Sanger in *The New Yorker*, writer Helena Huntington Smith noted that the *Woman Rebel*:

> . . . mixed its birth-control propaganda with a good deal of red-flag-waving, and perorations of the "Workers of the World, Arise!" variety. She printed rousing contributions entitled "A Defense of Assassination" and "The Song of the Bomb," and composed an editorial declaring: "Even if dynamite were to serve no other purpose than to call forth the spirit of revolutionary solidarity and loyalty, it would prove its great value."[2]

Because of content like this, Sanger was arraigned on federal charges of using the mails "to incite murder and assassination" and circulate "obscene" materials (that is, materials advocating contraception). The *Woman Rebel* folded after nine issues.

Her 1920 book, *Woman and the New Race*, was a manifesto of her revolutionary program to change the world. "Diplomats may formulate leagues of nations," she wrote, "and nations may pledge their utmost strength to maintain them . . . but woman, continuing to produce explosive populations, will convert these pledges into proverbial scraps of paper." On the other hand, "She may, by controlling birth, lift motherhood to the plane of a voluntary, intelligent function, and remake the world."[3]

Note that last phrase: "remake the world." Margaret Sanger belonged to the company of self-appointed social redeemers. A eugenicist, she believed that the world's problems—poverty, hunger, war—stemmed from the "fit" having too few children and the "unfit" having too many. The "unfit" were people of the lower classes and races she regarded as inferior. The disastrous situation that uncontrolled births created could be remedied, she believed, if people could be bred like animals with an eye to improving the species. She attributed the lack of proper breeding to the "sexual subservience" of women that allowed this to happen.

Focusing on women as the world's potential saviors, Sanger believed that salvation lay in "liberating" women by endowing them with "reproductive freedom," the ability to decide whether to have children or not. She wrote, "Even as birth control is the means by which woman attains basic freedom, so it is the means by which she must and will uproot the evil she has wrought through her submission."[4]

She based the title of her 1922 book *The Pivot of Civilization* on the notion that birth control is the pivot or turning point by which civilization can move from barbarism and disaster to future rationality and well-being.[5] Such delusional world-transforming ambitions lie at the heart of every radical cause and fuel the extremist energies and beliefs. "Reproductive freedom"—with its implications of world-transforming consequences—is still the rallying cry of the women's movement Sanger inspired.

"Penumbras" and "Emanations"

Defending the 1879 Connecticut contraception law, and opposing the radicals, stood the Catholic Church, a formidable power in the state. The Catholic case rested on its view that the use of contraception had a harmful effect on individuals and families. The church asserted that, by detaching sex from childbearing, contraception degraded marriage "since the husband and wife who indulge in any form of this practice come to have a lower idea of married life."[6]

The church also argued that legalizing contraceptives would break down the character and willpower of unmarried people, making it easier for them to give in to the urge for sex outside marriage and detached from procreation: "The deliberate restriction of the family through these immoral practices, weakens self-control and the capacity for self-denial, and increases the love of ease and luxury."[7]

These claims were rooted in observations about the behaviors of individuals, and could be argued and disputed. The disagreements could have been resolved in democratic forums, as the founders intended. In a representative democracy, contending parties are forced to compromise to resolve a dispute. Compromise leads to a more tranquil resolution of quarrels. The obvious remedy for a bad law or an obsolete law is to replace it with a better law.

The plaintiffs in *Griswold v. Connecticut* had already tried changing the law through the legislature. This course had failed because the reformers were too small a minority to overcome the church's influence. Estelle Griswold, Planned Parenthood, and the ACLU did not then embark on a campaign to persuade the people of Connecticut to press for repeal of the law. As radicals, they were pursuing more intoxicating goals: new rights to "reproductive freedom," "gender equality," the liberation of women. Such goals could not wait on the persuasion of a majority. Such goals justified an effort to impose them on the majority.

The radicals knew they had potential allies in the liberal justices who had earlier abolished school prayer without a clear precedent. And they were excited at the prospect, once again, of achieving a revolutionary goal simultaneously in all fifty states. Consequently, the Planned Parenthood legal team began developing a "constitutional" argument they could take to the Supreme Court. The argument they came up with claimed that the Connecticut law violated a constitutional "right to privacy."[8]

There was no such constitutional right. There is no mention in the Constitution of a right to privacy. Nor does the Constitution refer to sexual relations between men and women. But the legal team knew that the Court had played fast and loose with the Constitution in the prayer cases and pressed ahead. The plaintiff lawyers filed suit against the Connecticut law and proceeded to make their right-to-privacy argument.

In June 1965, the U.S. Supreme Court ruled by a majority of seven to two that the right to contraception was guaranteed by a "right to privacy," claiming that such a right could be found in the "penumbras" or shadows of other rights in the Constitution, even if the Constitution was mute on the subject itself. The Court agreed with the plaintiffs' argument and found the Connecticut law to be "unconstitutional."

This decision, and the reasoning behind it, produced much head-scratching among legal commentators. It was Justice William O. Douglas who wrote the majority opinion conceding that the Bill of Rights did not contain an explicit right to privacy. Nonetheless, he contended that the rights explicitly guaranteed in the Constitution had "penumbras," created by "emanations from these guarantees that help give them life and substance." According to Douglas, the "spirit" of the First Amendment (guaranteeing free speech), Third Amendment (prohibiting forced quartering of troops), Fourth Amendment (freedom from unreasonable searches and seizures), Fifth Amendment (freedom from self-incrimination), and Ninth Amendment as applied to the states by the Fourteenth Amendment, created a general "right to privacy" that could not be unduly infringed.[9]

Justices Hugo Black and Potter Stewart dissented from this tortured construction. Black emphasized the fact that the right to privacy was not in the Constitution, and he specifically criticized Douglas's interpretations of the Ninth and Fourteenth Amendments. Stewart observed that while the Connecticut statute was "an uncommonly silly law," it was nonetheless constitutional. The problem posed by the 1879 prohibition, he said, should properly have been addressed by changing the law, instead of a fundamental change in interpreting the Constitution.

But fundamental change was what the Court majority wanted. The *Griswold* decision applied only to married couples. But the discovery of a "right to privacy" in the "penumbras" and "emanations" of the Bill of Rights would provide a rationale for a series of new rights that would change the American landscape for generations to come: in 1972, the right to birth control for unmarried couples; in 1973, a woman's constitutional right to abortion; in 1977, a right to contraception for juveniles at least sixteen years of age; in 2002 a right to homosexual relations; and in 2015, a right to same-sex marriage.

Of these, the 1973 ruling in *Roe v. Wade* had by far the most dramatic and far-reaching impact.

The Issue Is Revolution

The *Roe v. Wade* decision was a logical extension of the fight over contraception. Leftists generally viewed abortion as simply another form of birth control, and another advance on the road to "women's liberation." But there's obviously a profound difference between abortion and contraception. Abortion involves another party: the unborn child.

Outside the Catholic community, *Griswold* and other rulings on contraception had provoked very little controversy. The *Roe v. Wade* abortion ruling, by contrast, divided the entire nation because it involved the sanctity of life itself. The abortion controversy created intensely passionate political factions on the left and right, whose battles are still raging nearly half a century later.

Pulitzer Prize–winning author David J. Garrow has written the definitive history of the campaign behind *Roe v. Wade*. In *Liberty and Sexuality: The Right to Privacy and the Making of Roe v. Wade*, he locates the origins of the decision in the activities of a few radical women at the University of Texas, members of the New Left organization Students for a Democratic Society (SDS).

The leader of this group contributed an article to Austin's leftist underground newspaper, the *Rag*. "We in Women's Liberation," she wrote, "deny any inherent differences between men and women. . . . All of us are trapped by the society that created our roles. We are questioning the ideals of marriage and motherhood . . . [and] the very society that has created these roles and values must also be questioned."[10]

The idea that people are "trapped" in roles that "society" imposes on them—like marriage and motherhood—is Marxist in origin. It takes away the choices that individuals make, e.g., what roles they should accept or reject or how they should conduct them. It subordinates questions like whether to have an abortion to grandiose abstractions like "patriarchal oppression" and "reproductive freedom," which eliminate individual circumstances and choices all together. Christians and Jews, and others not seduced by Marxist schemas of oppression and liberation, see individuals with free will who are responsible for their choices, which include whether to take the innocent life of an unborn child or not.

Saul Alinsky, the radical organizer and mentor of Barack Obama and Hillary Clinton, used to ask his new followers why they wanted to become community organizers. They would respond with idealistic claims that they wanted to help the poor and oppressed. Then Alinsky would scream at them like a Marine Corps drill instructor, "No! You want to organize for power!" That's the way the SDS radicals at the University of Texas approached the abortion issue—as a means to power, or, in Margaret Sanger's words, to remake the world. As a writer in the 1960s radical SDS publication *New Left Notes* put it, "The issue is never the issue. The issue is always the revolution."

The Sacrificial Lamb

Sarah Weddington was a graduate of the University of Texas Law School and a friend of the campus radicals. While in law school she had become pregnant, and because this would interfere with her career, she and her husband decided to abort the child. Since abortions were illegal in Texas, they traveled across the border to the Mexican town of Piedras Negras.

Part of the campus group's birth control project was counseling women on how to obtain Mexican abortions. They wanted Weddington to give them legal advice on whether giving this advice exposed their group to criminal prosecution. The discussions led rapidly to the idea of filing a Supreme Court suit.

To accomplish this, they needed a plaintiff—a woman who was already pregnant and needed an abortion for reasons the Court would find compelling. The problem was that most women who wanted an abortion wanted to get it over with as soon as possible. A court case, they knew, could take years. Weddington and her co-counsel found the plaintiff they were looking for in Norma McCorvey, who would become the "Jane Roe" of *Roe v. Wade*.

The twenty-two-year-old McCorvey had been married and divorced twice. She'd had a child by each husband and had passed both children on to be raised by relatives. Now she was pregnant again by a man she wasn't married to. She was desperate to get an abortion. Her life was in chaos. She was a drug abuser, homeless, sexually confused, emotionally unstable, and fragile.

Sarah Weddington's political goal was to make abortions as available as contraception, and she was willing to use any means necessary to do so, even offering to help a woman in dire circumstances and then betraying her. Because of the requirements of the legal case, instead of recommending an abortionist, Weddington persuaded the impressionable McCorvey *not* to abort her baby pending the Court's decision, even though she was well aware that McCorvey would deliver her baby long before the case was concluded. As it turned out, it took three years for the case to reach the Supreme Court. In the meantime, McCorvey gave birth to a girl and put her daughter up for adoption.

Years later, Norma McCorvey had a change of heart, renounced her role in *Roe v. Wade*, and joined the anti-abortion camp. In 1997 she wrote an account of what she felt was the shabby treatment she had received from Weddington and her feminist colleagues:

> Though Sarah had passed herself off as my friend, in reality she used me. When I sat down with her and discussed the possibility of getting an abortion, Sarah knew where I could get one because she had gotten one herself three years before. When I asked her if the court's decision would come in time for me to get an abortion, she gave an evasive answer. And she did so with full understanding that it would come way too late to help me. If Sarah Weddington was so interested in abortion, why didn't she tell me where she got hers? Because I was of no use to her unless I was pregnant.[11]

Weddington's behavior outraged even a pro-abortion reporter for the *Texas Observer*, who wrote: "By not effectively informing [Norma] of [where she could get an abortion], the feminists who put together *Roe v. Wade* turned her into Choice's sacrificial lamb."

McCorvey agreed with that assessment, saying, "I never signed up to be a sacrificial lamb for anyone; I was just a young woman who needed help and turned to the wrong people. After I gave up my child for adoption, I spent years searching the faces of children I passed on the streets and in supermarkets. *Is that her?* I'd ask myself. *Could that be my child?*"[12]

On the Front Lines

When the *Roe v. Wade* decision was announced, it had a familiar ring—and a familiar majority ruling of seven to two. Once again the newly invented "right of privacy" formed the basis of the majority opinion, written this time by Justice Harry Blackmun: "This right of privacy, whether it be founded in the Fourteenth Amendment's concept of personal liberty and restrictions upon state action, as we feel it is, or, as the District Court determined, in the Ninth Amendment's reservation of rights to the people, is broad enough to encompass a woman's decision whether or not to terminate her pregnancy."[13]

The liberal media, led by the *New York Times*, applauded the *Roe* decision, as they had *Griswold* and the Madalyn Murray result before. Dissent from the Court bench and from legal scholars, on the other hand, was as harsh as it had been when *Griswold* first invoked the right-to-privacy claim. One dissenter, Justice Rehnquist, pointed out that even if the Constitution contained a right to privacy—and it didn't—an abortion was hardly a private act.[14] Justice White wrote, "I find nothing in the language or history of the Constitution to support the Court's judgment." Renowned Yale legal scholar John Hart Ely—a *supporter* of legal abortion—dismissed the Court's decision in this withering commentary:

> What is unusual about *Roe* is that the liberty involved is accorded . . . a protection more stringent, I think it is fair to say, than that the present Court accords the freedom of the press explicitly guaranteed by the First Amendment. What is frightening about *Roe* is that this super-protected right, is not inferable from the language of the Constitution, the framers' thinking respecting the specific problem in issue, any general value derivable from the provisions they included or the nation's governmental structure. . . . It is bad because it is bad constitutional law, or rather because it is not constitutional law, and gives almost no sense of an obligation to try to be.[15]

In case after case—religious expression in schools, contraception, abortion—the Supreme Court handed down a string of earthshaking decisions founded on the flimsiest and even bogus constitutional reasoning. The unintended consequence of these decisions was to place the Supreme Court on the front lines of an epic culture war. It was not merely a war between right and left, but between secularism and religion, especially the Christian religion. The secular left had discovered an all-powerful instrument—the Supreme Court—with which it could impose its radical, anti-Christian agenda on an unwilling nation.

When Ronald Reagan was elected president in 1980, he was supported by a newly energized religious right. Reagan was determined to nominate Supreme Court justices who shared his anti-*Roe* views. "I feel very strongly about those social issues," he said, "but I also place my confidence in the fact that the one thing that I do seek are judges that will interpret the law and not write the law. We've had too many examples in recent years of courts and judges legislating."[16]

Judge Bork—a Casualty of the War

In 1987, Reagan nominated the conservative judge Robert Bork to the Court. Bork had a stellar reputation as one of the nation's most brilliant legal minds and constitutional experts. After reviewing his credentials, the American Bar Association had given him its highest rating.[17] Until that moment, presidential nominees were normally passed pro forma through their Senate confirmation hearings if they showed ample knowledge of the law and did not have disqualifying character issues.

But within 45 minutes of Bork's nomination, the leading Senate Democrat, Ted Kennedy, launched a vicious attack on his character and judgment, wholly unprecedented in the annals of Supreme Court appointments. On July 1, 1987, Kennedy spoke from the Senate floor and made one outrageous statement after another, including these defamatory lies:

> Robert Bork's America is a land in which women would be forced into back-alley abortions, blacks would sit at

segregated lunch counters, rogue police could break down citizens' doors in midnight raids, and schoolchildren could not be taught about evolution, writers and artists could be censored at the whim of the Government, and the doors of the Federal courts would be shut on the fingers of millions of citizens.[18]

Kennedy's gutter attack was a calculated first strike that kicked off a multimillion-dollar leftist campaign to block the Bork appointment. This in itself was an unprecedented assault on the constitutional process, which has warped Court nomination proceedings ever since.

The day before Bork's nomination, forty-five left-wing organizations met with Kennedy in the office of the Leadership Conference on Civil Rights. They issued a joint statement labeling Bork an "ultraconservative" and claiming his confirmation would "jeopardize the civil rights achievements of the past three decades."[19] The leftist coalition labeled Bork a "racist" and a "sexist" and lied about his legal views. In national television and newspaper ads, in mailings and press releases, they lied about his character, called him an "ideological extremist" and a pawn of the wealthy, and pronounced him unfit to be a Supreme Court justice.

There was nothing in Judge Bork's long public career to justify these charges. Former Chief Justice Warren Burger said, "I do not think in more than fifty years since I was in law school there has ever been a nomination of a man or woman any better qualified than Judge Bork."[20] He had been Solicitor General of the United States in the Nixon administration, a circuit judge on the D.C. Circuit Court of Appeals (the second most important court in the land), and a nationally respected law professor at Yale.

Judge Bork had sat on the D.C. Circuit with Antonin Scalia and voted in concert with him 98 percent of the time. Scalia had already been confirmed to a Supreme Court seat without a dissenting vote. Yet Planned Parenthood took out a full-page ad in papers across the country, calling Bork "an ultra-conservative judicial extremist." The American Civil Liberties Union sent an urgent fund-raising telegram to supporters, alleging that "detailed research reveals Bork far more dangerous than previously believed.... We risk nothing short of wrecking the entire Bill of Rights.... His confirmation would threaten our entire system of government."[21]

For twenty-five years, ever since the 1962 decision on school prayer, the Supreme Court had been the all-powerful lever that a radical minority had used to impose its will on the majority. That judicial lever had radically reinterpreted and twisted the Constitution to fit the leftist agenda. Judge Bork was an "originalist," a legal scholar who believed in interpreting the Constitution as it was written. He opposed engaging in judicial activism and legislating from the bench. The left feared that Robert Bork's confirmation would threaten its control of the Supreme Court and take away that lever—and possibly overturn or limit *Roe v. Wade*.

So, led by Senator Ted Kennedy, the left pulled out all the stops to destroy Bork's reputation. The scurrilous attacks on his character were intended to mobilize Democratic constituents through fear (especially black voters), even before the confirmation hearings began. The smear campaign worked. Bork's nomination was rejected by the Democrat-controlled Senate, 58 to 42. Only two Democrats voted to confirm.

The Judge Bork episode reflects the nature of the war the radicals are waging against religious liberty and Christian America. The left—and this has come to include the Democratic senators who sit on the judiciary committee—has no conscience or restraint when it comes to destroying people who stand in its way. The war began with the removal of the religious presence from America's public schools. Since then, it has only grown more divisive and intense.

8

Battle Lines

WHEN DR. DOLORES BERNADETTE Grier died on February 22, 2018, three communities mourned—the pro-life community, the Catholic community, and the African-American community. The founder of the Association of Black Catholics Against Abortion, Dr. Grier was inspired to oppose abortion in 1977 after hearing a speech by civil rights leader Jesse Jackson. After his speech, she went up to him and said, "Reverend Jackson, I'm going to join the pro-life movement. You said the pro-life movement needed youth and color, and I am the color."

Dolores Grier deeply admired Reverend Jackson's position as a black pro-life Democrat. In an interview published two months after the *Roe v. Wade* decision, Reverend Jackson told

Jet magazine, "Abortion is genocide. . . . Anything growing is living."[1] Dolores Grier was heartbroken years later when Reverend Jackson sought the support of the hard-left wing of the Democratic Party for his presidential run—and reversed his stance on abortion.

Dr. Grier gave a speech in 1989 for the American Life League, saying:

> Abortion is racism. It is a way of pruning, if you will, the black population. . . . In 1973, shortly after the civil rights struggles, when there were more benefits for black people, all of a sudden we were given this free, free thing from the society of America: abortion. Seventy-eight percent of your free abortion clinics were placed in black and urban areas, for the purpose of something free of charge from a racist society. To put it in the words of one pro-abortionist, "We don't need so many Negroes anymore. There's no more cotton to pick."[2]

Dr. Grier joined an exodus of Democrats from a party they and their families had been committed to for generations.

Threatened and Besieged

By ending traditions and practices that went back to the founding of the nation, by reversing even longer-standing moral attitudes, and by doing so overnight, the Supreme Court had produced an earthquake in the political landscape. By establishing new moral codes based on questionable interpretations of the Constitution and inserting them into the very foundations of the nation; by imposing them simultaneously on every precinct, in every city and state in the Union, regardless of whether their inhabitants were sympathetic to the new codes or not, nine politically appointed justices had declared war on everyone who viewed the changes as assaults on their identities as Americans, or on their fundamental religious beliefs, or simply on their membership in communities that did not approve of those changes.

In a dissent from one of the Supreme Court's post-*Roe* abortion decisions, Justice Scalia rightly observed: "[By] foreclosing all democratic outlets for the deep passions this issue arouses, by banishing the issue from the political forum that gives all participants, even the losers, the satisfaction of a fair hearing and an honest fight, by continuing the imposition of a rigid national rule instead of allowing for regional differences, the Court merely prolongs and intensifies the anguish."[3] Over the years, that anguish has hardened into resistance, and Americans have become divided not only over particular issues but over the fundamental laws of the nation itself, and—even more ominously—over what it means to be an American.

These Supreme Court decisions and the politics that inspired them were assaults on American pluralism, on the diversity of American communities, and on the fundamental American principles of equality and religious liberty. The Court itself, however, is only an instrument. The force behind the assaults was a radical movement whose members are convinced the society-transforming ends justify the undemocratic and extra-constitutional and even racist means. Their legal teams marched the issues through the courts and shaped the arguments—especially the invented "right to privacy"—to take advantage of an authority that could impose their minority agendas on an entire nation.

The *Roe* decision divided the nation along ideological, cultural, and even geographical fault lines. The pro-abortion camp was radical and cosmopolitan, concentrated on the two liberal coasts (especially New York and Hollywood); and it was represented in left-wing organizations and institutions like the ACLU, Planned Parenthood, the National Abortion and Reproductive Rights Action League, the Democratic Party, academia, and the news media.

On the pro-life side were Americans who resided in a more rural and religious America, centered in the Bible Belt, but including Catholic urban areas. These communities felt directly assaulted by *Roe* and the radical forces behind it, and experienced this threat to their own communities as viscerally as they did the threat from the Communists in the ongoing cold war.

NO ROOM FOR COMPROMISE

The *Roe* decision provoked a seismic public reaction. The Second Vatican Council had already condemned abortion as "an unspeakable crime" in 1962. So it was no surprise that, within months of the 1973 *Roe v. Wade* decision, the Catholic Church founded the "right-to-life" movement. The National Conference of Catholic Bishops declared that "a moral imperative" existed for a "well-planned and coordinated political organization by citizens at the national, state and local levels."[4] The goal of the movement was to add a right-to-life amendment to the Constitution.

The immediate result of the church's demarche was to destroy the political coalition that had created the New Deal and powered the Democratic Party to electoral victories for three generations. In his book *Left at the Altar*, Democratic Party centrist Michael Winters explored the political schism caused by *Roe v. Wade*. "Abortion," Winters wrote, "was the iceberg against which the New Deal coalition of Catholics and liberals sank."[5]

It wasn't merely the abortion issue that sank the coalition ship. The coalition was destroyed by the offensive and demeaning arguments put forth by the defenders of *Roe*, especially the radical feminists. They hailed *Roe* as a victory in the feminist battle to overthrow the existing order. The radicals' demands were framed in such an aggressive and offensive way that a split became inevitable.

Michael Winters observed, "Catholics heard echoes of anti-Catholic bigotry and of eugenics in the arguments for liberalizing abortion laws, echoes that...were disturbing and unwelcome."[6] One particularly offensive attack was leveled by feminist icon Florynce Kennedy, who said, "If men could get pregnant, abortion would be a sacrament."[7] The word "sacrament" was a calculated attack on Catholics' beliefs, in a sentence that accused them of misogyny.

More important was the series of nonnegotiable claims underlying all the feminist arguments: Abortion is just another form of contraception. A woman has a right to control her own body, regardless of the decisions that caused her pregnancy or the rights of the unborn child. To the feminists, abortion is the cornerstone of "gender equality" and women's liberation. An unborn fetus is not a baby, not a person, but merely a blob of tissue, part of the woman's body. These feminist arguments removed the unborn child from consideration entirely, a position that left no room for compromise or even dialogue.

Radical Aggression Against Religion

In 1968, the Democratic Party had adopted one of its equality-of-outcomes socialist rules, requiring that 50 percent of delegates to its national convention be women regardless of whether they merited the status of being a delegate. This gave the feminists the leverage to force the party to accept their extreme views as the party line. The religious fervor of the radical feminist position was expressed by Catholic feminist Mary Daly:

> The repeal of anti-abortion laws should be seen within the wide context of the oppression of women in sexual hierarchical society. . . . The women's movement is bringing into being a new consciousness, which is beginning to challenge the symbols and ethics of patriarchal religion. The transvaluation of values which is beginning to take place affects not only thinking on abortion, but *the whole spectrum of moral questions*.[8] [Emphasis added]

In other words, according to Daly and her followers, feminism is here to replace traditional religion, which is reactionary and oppressive. The term "transvaluation" announces the revolutionary nature of their project. It intends to abolish traditional religion, which requires the subordination and oppression of women, and replace it with a feminist religion, to whom people will now look for the answers to moral questions. This is heady stuff, but hardly the kind of think-ing that would allow dialogue between the parties. "We will eliminate you" is not a negotiating position.

Prior to *Roe*, there had been many debates about abortion across the country. Should abortion be permitted in cases of rape or incest? In cases of fetal abnormality? What should abortion law be for the people of New York and California? For the people of Kansas and Georgia? Should ending the life of an unborn child be left to the mother's whim, or should there be specific circumstances and time frames in which abortion might be an acceptable course?

These and many other questions were the subject of dia-logues before *Roe*—but *Roe* ended thoughtful discussion and compromise. Michael Winters, writing from the perspective of a concerned Democrat and Catholic, lamented how this avenue had been closed:

> Democrats could have responded to *Roe* in a variety of ways. They could have worked to make adoption procedures less cumbersome or fought to extend healthcare benefits to help women whose economic circumstances might incline them to seek the relatively less expensive alternative of an abortion.... They could have supported a constitutional amendment turn-ing the issue back to the states where it had been before *Roe*. Any of these approaches would have better reflected the pub-lic's persistent ambivalence about abortion. Instead the party leadership largely bought the feminists' interpretation of *Roe*.[9]

Of course, it wasn't just an *interpretation* of *Roe* that the Democrats adopted. The party bought into the idea that women should be morally autonomous and freed of any responsibility toward their pregnancy. The feminist-invented constitutional "right to privacy" negated the unborn child's right to life—and conferred a near-absolute right for a woman to have an abortion without consulting anyone, including the father of the unborn child.

Before *Roe*, the Democratic Party had been divided on abortion. But the *Roe* decision made it virtually impossible for any party official to hold a pro-life position. In a letter to a prominent Catholic two years earlier, Senator Ted Kennedy had written, "Once life has begun, no matter at what stage of growth, it is my belief that termination should not be decided merely by desire."[10] After the *Roe* decision was handed down, Kennedy was forced to become one of the defenders of a woman's right to abort her baby, based solely on her desire to do so.

Like many other Catholic Democratic Party leaders, Kennedy sought to avoid the charge of hypocrisy by claiming that, in his private beliefs as a Catholic, he was still opposed to abortion.[11] Once pro-choice policy was established as the official Democratic Party position, pro-life Catholics who were unwilling to surrender their principles (as Ted Kennedy had) migrated in droves to the Republican camp.

Energized by the *Roe* decision, the left stepped up its radical aggressions against the religious community. Each victory motivated the leftists to move on to the next item on their expansive agenda. The issue was never the issue. The issue was always the revolution. Each radical victory only inspired more radical aspirations and efforts.

How the Left Created the Religious Right

The next agenda item after *Roe* was the Equal Rights Amendment (ERA). The Equal Rights Amendment to the Constitution was introduced in 1971. It was approved by the Democratic-controlled House on October 12, 1971, and by the Democratic-controlled Senate on March 22, 1972, the year before the *Roe* decision. By 1977 the ERA had been endorsed by Presidents Nixon, Ford, and Carter and ratified by 35 of the 38 states required to pass it.

Written by feminists, the proposed amendment would have erased all legal distinctions between men and women. It was stopped just short of passage when Phyllis Schlafly mobilized a successful grassroots movement of conservative women. Schlafly pointed out that since the Constitution didn't refer to women or men but to "we the people," its equal rights protections already included women. On the other hand, the ERA's denial of any differences between the sexes would strip women of rights they already had, including rights involving marriage and divorce. The ERA might even make women subject to the military draft.[12]

The left's attempt to change the social order and marginalize religion provoked a national resistance movement. The radicals had successfully pushed their agenda through the Supreme Court and had nearly achieved their grand objective: amending the United States Constitution. But their impatience was their undoing. By attempting to achieve sweeping social change without persuading the country, precinct by precinct, through the democratic process, the left had created a resistance that was national in scope.

Driven by its desire to transform the social order, the left's aggressions had frightened and offended Catholics and other religious conservatives. Among the unintended consequences was not only to drive Catholics into the Republican Party but to forge a pro-life alliance of Catholics and Protestants. This new spirit of Catholic-Protestant unity was reflected in a statement by a prominent, liberal Protestant theologian: "The Catholic Church is here defending the very frontier of what constitutes the mystery of our being. . . . Next to the issue of peace in the world, I feel the opposition to abortion and euthanasia constitutes the second major moral issue of our society (racial integration and the preservation of the family being third and fourth)."[13]

Prior to *Roe*, Baptists and evangelicals had not been politically active as a bloc. Jerry Falwell, head of the newly formed Moral Majority and one of the most important leaders of the religious right, said he had previously thought "the separation doctrine was to keep the church out of politics."[14] But once the communities of the Bible Belt came under siege from the left, conservative Christians changed their attitudes on political involvement. The Moral Majority, one of the most powerful new religious right organizations, defined its politics as "pro-life," "pro-traditional family," "pro-morality," and "pro-American." At its height, Falwell's movement claimed 4 million members.[15]

The school prayer decision had already stimulated a dramatic growth of Christian schools, plus an increase in the number of parents choosing to homeschool their children. A 1978 attempt by the IRS to revoke tax-exempt status for Christian schools encountered overwhelming resistance and was quickly withdrawn. It was, as one observer wrote, "'the precise trigger' for the rise of the religious right."[16] Christians felt that their families, churches, and beliefs were under siege. The attacks on their religion by the government and the left galvanized them to seek the political means to defend themselves.

Within six years of the *Roe* decision, a new and powerful religious right had entered the political arena to defend the moral concerns of the Christian faith. These groups focused heavily on the family, the core institution they saw threatened by the newly radicalized moral order. Among its leading organizations were the American Family Association, formed in 1977, Focus on the Family (1979), Concerned Women of America (1979), and the Moral Majority (1979).

Their views, forged in battles with the left, were a natural fit with conservative politics, producing a shift to the right within the Republican Party. Under pressure from the religious right, the Republican Party withdrew its support for the Equal Rights Amendment and instead called for the restoration of prayer in public schools. The religious right was a major force in securing the nomination of Ronald Reagan, and registered millions of new voters to push Reagan over the top in the 1980 presidential election. Reagan adopted the Christian right's opposition to abortion, and his traditional-values rhetoric resonated with the Christian right's moral views.

Pressure from the religious right motivated state governments to pass laws limiting the right to abortion—laws requiring parental consent; spousal notification laws; requirements that abortions be performed in hospitals rather than clinics;

laws barring state funding for abortions; and bans on "partial birth abortions" (a horrifying procedure, morally indistinguishable from infanticide, in which babies in late-term pregnancies undergo a partial delivery and are killed). Some (but not all) of these state restrictions were struck down by the Supreme Court.

The radical assaults on Christian values and morality did not let up; nor did their defeats cause radicals to rethink their maximalist demands. The passion that galvanized the left was not about changing particular laws and institutions or solving specific social problems. It was about changing *the world*.

Freedom from Responsibility

What Christians experienced as a war against their families, their communities, and their values was the result of the left's "transformative" agendas. The motivating ideas of the leftist offensive brooked no compromise. If the right to abortion was part of a plan to replace traditional religion and its values in ways that would affect "not only thinking on abortion but the whole spectrum of moral questions," what room was there for compromise with their religious opponents? It was a prescription for conflicts that were irreconcilable.

The radical position left opponents with no moral ground to occupy. Thus, the feminist claim that abortion rights must be viewed "within the wide context of the oppression of women in sexual hierarchical society" cast opponents of abortion as "oppressors." This removed those who disagreed with the feminist view from the community of voices concerned about the welfare of women. It dismissed their arguments without considering them. They were "sexist" and "anti-woman." If opponents of abortion are viewed as anti-woman, their concerns for the 60 million babies that have been aborted since *Roe v. Wade* are morally tainted.

Within the ranks of the left, discussions of the social impacts of the feminist position were rendered impossible. Consider the harm feminist positions caused in the African American community. According to the New York City Department of Health and Mental Hygiene, in 2013 more African American babies were aborted (29,007) than were born (24,758) in the city.[17] Why is a discussion of this off-limits among leftists? Because any suggestion that abortion causes social harm is an attack on women's "reproductive freedom," and thus on women, and thus morally reprehensible.

Feminists mobilize their supporters behind the "right to choose," which they claim is necessary to establish the absolute autonomy of the liberated woman. "Pro-choice," the banner under which they march, means the unconditional right to an abortion, a concept that implies a liberation from biology and its consequences, and from any moral obligations associated with the ability to bear children.

But there is a sleight of hand in the slogan itself. Before making the choice to have an abortion, a woman makes many other choices that radicals simply ignore: There is the choice to have sex and the choice of whom to have sex with. There is the choice to get pregnant and the choice that led to getting pregnant. Or to remaining pregnant until an abortion becomes the only way to terminate the pregnancy. Ever since the introduction of the "morning-after pill," women have had a "plan B" available to prevent fertilization from taking place up to three days after intercourse.

Moreover, there has always been another choice available that radical feminists don't like to talk about: The choice to give life to the child through adoption. This is a positive choice that the pro-abortion movement never speaks of. What feminists are actually demanding is not, in fact, the freedom to choose. They are demanding to be free from responsibility for their choices.

Breaking the Social Contract

When the Supreme Court circumvented the democratic process and imposed its will on America through *Roe* and similar decisions, it led to unintended consequences that went far beyond the abortion question. These decisions struck at the very core of America's social contract. Prior to *Roe*, postwar America had been remarkably successful in maintaining a stable, cohesive society that was multiethnic, multiracial, multireligious, and free. By shattering a common understanding of our most basic social contract—the Constitution—the Court drove a stake through the heart of the foundation that has held Americans together.

In those years since World War II, America saw remarkable changes in social attitudes—some so dramatic that no one could have predicted them. For example, in the era of segregation, there was no more volatile racial issue than sexual encounters between blacks and whites. Anthropologists regard attitudes toward interracial marriage as a key index of a society's assimilation of its minorities. In 1958, only 4 percent of white Americans approved of interracial marriages between blacks and whites. By 2013, the approval figure had jumped to 87 percent.[18] Over the years, black-and-white couples have become ubiquitous in public life and popular culture, on television shows and even in commercials, whose producers take special care not to use images that might offend and alienate customers.

Interracial sexual relationships that once could have provoked lynchings are now accepted as normal. How did this happen? There was no Supreme Court decision that declared interracial marriage to be a constitutional right. This result was achieved through years of conversation and persuasion throughout our culture. Attitudes changed as all Americans came to accept that black Americans are included in America's social contract, which requires that all citizens be treated with dignity as equals.

Jerry Falwell, the founder of the Moral Majority, was once a committed segregationist, as were many members of the religious right in the Bible Belt. Many Christian leaders in the South had resisted the Supreme Court's 1954 decision to end segregation in the public schools. But in the 1960s, Falwell's attitude changed. He had hired an Indonesian musician of dark complexion for his music ministry at the Thomas Road Baptist Church, which he had founded. When some parishioners objected, he stood firm and kept the new man on staff.

In 1968 Thomas Road Baptist Church accepted its first black members. In 1969 Falwell's Lynchburg Christian Academy accepted its first black student. Falwell had experienced a conversion: "I realized that I was completely wrong, that what I had been taught was completely wrong," he said.

"For me it was a scriptural and personal realization that segregation was evil. I realized it was not taught in the Bible."[19]

For over 225 years, democratic persuasion—a process made possible by the First Amendment, and by government through the consent of the governed—is what has made the American social contract work. Americans talked about their differences, listened to one another, and debated and compromised. It was all made possible by mutual respect for the right of others to dissent and disagree. This is the process to which radicals have laid siege.

9

A Radical Epidemic

IN THE EARLY MORNING hours of June 28, 1969, New York City police raided the Stonewall Inn, a gay bar on Christopher Street in Greenwich Village. Police raids were a common occurrence at the Stonewall Inn, and the bar patrons usually cooperated with police. This night was different.

The patrons threw coins and bottles at police and refused to disperse. The commotion spilled out onto Christopher Street and attracted a crowd of onlookers. As arrests were made, a crowd of more than 400 people heckled and jeered the police. In minutes, the protest escalated into a violent clash in the street. Some protesters taunted the police with shouts of "Gay power!" That night, police arrested thirteen people, and dozens more were hospitalized.

The next night, a crowd again gathered in front of the Stonewall Inn. When police arrived, people shouted and chanted in protest. The gatherings clogged Christopher Street for six nights in a row. One of those nights again turned violent, causing numerous injuries. These events became known as the Stonewall Riots, and the site of the Stonewall Inn is considered the birthplace of the LGBT rights movement. "From the ashes of the Stonewall Riots," boasted Mark Segal, one of the participants, "we created the Gay Liberation Front."[1]

The Gay Liberation Front (GLF) took its name from the Vietnamese National Liberation Front, the official name of the Vietnamese Communist Viet Cong. This new movement would soon become as fierce an antagonist to the religious right (and vice versa) as the radical feminists. Eager to expand the gay rights community and increase its power, the Gay Liberation Front issued a manifesto of the movement's goals: "We are a revolutionary homosexual group of men and women formed with the realization that complete liberation of all people cannot come about unless existing social institutions are abolished."[2] It was another grandiose leftist plan to reshape society and remake the world.

Sex with Strangers as a Revolutionary Act

The radicals defined gay liberation not as the inclusion of gay Americans into the existing social contract, but as the destruction of that contract. As the central symbol of their revolt, gay radicals practiced a defiant promiscuity. It was an in-your-face challenge to what they regarded as a repressive "sex-negative" culture. Gay radicals believed that monogamous marriage and the nuclear family were tyrannical structures imposed on them by their heterosexual "oppressors." Their name for this oppression was "heteronormativity," and they set out to overthrow it.

In the view of gay radicals, existing sexual prohibitions reflected no lessons drawn from humanity's biological realities and moral experience; they were merely "social constructions" imposed by an oppressive culture. Consequently, gay liberators did not seek civic tolerance, respect, and integration into the public order of "bourgeois" life. On the contrary, they were determined to do away with traditional middle-class standards of morality, sexual restraint, and even public hygiene.

The effect of this radical agenda was immediate and devastating. At the height of the sixties, during the flowering of the sexual revolution, doctors saw the incidence of amebiasis, a parasitic sexually transmitted disease, increase *fifty times* in San Francisco, a center of gay life. The reason for this outbreak was promiscuous sex among gays.[3] During the next decade, a tolerant American society retreated, while the sexual revolutionaries advanced. By the end of the seventies, two-thirds of gay men had already contracted hepatitis B.[4] Yet criticism of gay sexual practices on any grounds whatsoever—including public health concerns—was immediately condemned as "homophobic," a form of "racist" prejudice against gays.

Accommodating public officials licensed sexual gymnasiums called "bathhouses" and turned a blind eye toward public sex activity, including hookups between strangers in bookstore backrooms, bars, and "gloryhole" establishments.

A $100 million public sex industry flourished by decade's end. Gay activists described the sex establishments as gay "liberated zones."

One intellectual theorist of the movement, NYU professor Michael Warner, explained: "The phenomenology of a sex club encounter is an experience of *world making*. It's an experience of being connected not just to this person but to potentially limitless numbers of people, and that is why it's important that it be with a stranger"[5] [emphasis added]. Warner was the leader of an organization called "Sex Panic!," a name implying that anyone who thought that public sex with hundreds or thousands of strangers might be dangerous was merely having a panic attack caused by "sex-negative" prudery.

Calculated to Provoke the Religious Right

As the gay epidemics metastasized, nature began to assert itself with ever more devastating results. Opportunistic but treatable infections flourished in the petri dish of the liberated culture, as gay radicals went on with their defiant acts. Even the overloaded venereal disease clinics became trysting places in the liberated culture.

In his authoritative history of the AIDS epidemic, gay reporter Randy Shilts described the atmosphere in the liberated zones on the eve of the AIDS outbreak:

> Gay men were being washed by tide after tide of increasingly serious infections. First it was syphilis and gonorrhea. Gay men made up about 80% of the 70,000 annual patient visits to [San Francisco's] VD clinics. Easy treatment had imbued

them with such a cavalier attitude toward venereal diseases that many gay men saved their waiting-line numbers, like little tokens of desirability, and the clinic was considered an easy place to pick up both a shot and a date.[6]

Far from causing radical activists to rethink their agenda, the burgeoning epidemics prompted them to escalate their assault. When Dr. Dan William, a gay specialist, warned of the danger of continued promiscuity, he was publicly denounced as a "monogamist" in the gay press. When playwright Larry Kramer issued a similar warning, he was accused in the *New York Native* of "gay homophobia and anti-eroticism."

At a public meeting in the year preceding the first AIDS cases, Edmund White, coauthor of *The Joy of Gay Sex,* proposed that "gay men should wear their sexually transmitted diseases like red badges of courage in a war against a sex-negative society." Michael Callen, a gay youth present at the meeting, had already had 3,000 sexual partners and was shortly to come down with AIDS. When he heard White's triumphant defiance of the laws of nature, he thought, "Every time I get the clap I'm striking a blow for the sexual revolution."[7]

Callen later founded People With AIDS, and, in a courageously candid reflection, wrote:

Unfortunately, as a function of a microbiological...certainty, this level of sexual activity resulted in concurrent epidemics of syphilis, gonorrhea, hepatitis, amoebiasis, venereal warts and, we discovered too late, other pathogens. Unwittingly, and with the best of revolutionary intentions, a small subset of gay men managed to create disease settings equivalent to those of poor third-world nations in one of the richest nations on earth.[8]

Nor did the diseases remain stable. The enteric diseases—amebiasis, gay bowel syndrome, giardiasis, and shigellosis—were followed by an epidemic of hepatitis B, which Randy Shilts called "a disease that had transformed itself, via the popularity of anal intercourse, from a blood-borne scourge into a venereal disease."[9] The hepatitis B virus was transmitted in exactly the same way as the newly identified AIDS virus.

While these epidemics were progressing, the political leaders of the gay community held gay pride parades in major cities like Chicago, San Francisco, and New York. The theme of these parades reflected the liberation ethos of the movement. Half-naked (and sometimes fully naked) men brazenly flaunted their sexuality for maximum shock effect—a deliberate attempt to offend and affront what they regarded as the reactionary culture of the time.

These flamboyant displays of gay liberation persisted for twenty years, inspiring a satiric critique by the liberal website The Onion, "Gay-Pride Parade Sets Mainstream Acceptance of Gays Back 50 Years." The article quotes an imaginary straight female who witnesses a gay pride march in Los Angeles, remarking, "I'd always thought gays were regular people, just like you and me, and that the stereotype of homosexuals as hedonistic, sex-crazed deviants was just a destructive myth. Boy, oh, boy, was I wrong."[10]

Flaunting one's sexuality was considered a revolutionary act. The gay liberation activists were not merely trying to get attention or offend heterosexual society, or, more importantly, to persuade society to accept them as individuals on their own terms. They were trying to change the world by forcing *society* to accept aggressive public sexuality and, more importantly, promiscuous sexual behavior.

The political effect of these public displays of hedonism was the equivalent of a Supreme Court decision overthrowing tradition and precedent. They were calculated to provoke extreme reactions from the religious right. And they did.

A Clash of Hatreds

The leading religious opponent of gay liberation was Moral Majority founder Jerry Falwell. He said, "AIDS is not just God's punishment for homosexuals; it is God's punishment for the society that tolerates homosexuals."[11] It was a statement bigoted and un-Christian. Similar views were expressed by other vocal leaders of the religious right, while the majority of believers, however repugnant they found these antics, observed the Christian creed to "love the sinner but hate the sin."

The loud and confrontational voices of the gay radicals were also a minority within the gay community, albeit a large and active one. Most gay people had no interest in taking part in gay pride parades. They just wanted to be accepted and go about their lives. But to much of society, the antagonistic gay activists were the face of gay liberation. They were the leaders—and their rhetoric was no less hateful, deplorable, and intimidating than Falwell's.

Larry Kramer, a prominent gay writer and activist, was an opponent of such radical organizations as Michael Warner's Sex Panic! But like many of his peers, Kramer blamed the

Republican president for the epidemic. Kramer was well aware that Reagan had been elected with the support of the religious right, which he regarded as the oppressor enemy. "Ronald Reagan may have done laudable things," Kramer said, "but he was also a monster and, in my estimation, responsible for more deaths than Adolf Hitler."[12] This was the expression of an extreme and baseless hatred all too common on the left.

There was little that Ronald Reagan could have done to stop the epidemic. He was so hated and mocked by the left that any attempt to speak about the AIDS epidemic would have meant entering a political minefield. The claim that he didn't provide enough money for research was a canard, since public health officials already knew before they isolated the virus that HIV was transmitted like hepatitis B, which meant that unprotected anal sex with strangers was an extremely dangerous practice.

Members of the Reagan administration also demonstrated genuine concern for the victims of the epidemic. In 1983, still early in its progress, Reagan's Secretary of Health and Human Services, Margaret Heckler, made a publicized visit to the hospital bedside of a forty-year-old gay man dying of AIDS. Not only was Heckler the top-ranking health official in the Reagan administration; she was a devout Catholic. She held the man's hand out of compassion—and also to calm public fears that the disease might be spread by casual contact. Afterward she said, "We ought to be comforting the sick, rather than afflicting them and making them a class of outcasts."[13]

The only institution in a position to arrest the AIDS contagion at that time was the public health system. But public health officials were already under attack by gay radicals as instruments of the "sex-negative" society. Health officials were well aware that the gay bathhouses were a breeding ground for the various infections that ravaged the gay community. But fear of attacks from gay activists caused officials to take a hands-off policy toward the bathhouses.

Thus, an outbreak of herpes in the early seventies was a sufficient cause for public health officials to close heterosexual sex clubs like Plato's Retreat. But gay sex clubs, which were spreading far more dangerous diseases, were left open. The reason was the revolution. Gay bathhouses were "symbols of gay liberation from a sex-negative society," as one prominent activist put it.[14] When health officials suggested that gay people could protect themselves by practicing "safer sex," the gay left responded with hostility, calling the officials "homophobes," "bigots," and "Nazis."

The radical harassment campaigns succeeded, and the bathhouses remained open. The enforcement of traditional public health practices had been rendered politically impossible. Consequently, the epidemic continued to spread, and young gay men continued to die.

The Myth of the "Equal Opportunity Virus"

I coauthored of one of the early articles on AIDS in 1983.[15] When I interviewed Don Francis, the Centers for Disease Control official in charge of fighting both the hepatitis B and AIDS epidemics, he explained why public health officials didn't close the bathhouses during the epidemics that preceded AIDS in the 1960s and 1970s. "We didn't intervene," he told me, "because we felt that it would be interfering with an alternative lifestyle."[16] I understood what he really meant. He didn't want his agency to be picketed and attacked as homophobic, and he didn't want gay activists calling the health officials Nazis.

In 1983 when the article appeared, the AIDS epidemic was still confined to three cities with large homosexual communities: San Francisco, Los Angeles, and New York. At the time, the number of AIDS carriers was small enough that aggressive public health methods might have prevented the outward spread of the contagion. But every effort to take normal precautionary measures was thwarted by the political juggernaut that the gay liberation movement had created.

All three epicenters of the epidemic were controlled by the Democratic Party. Gay radicals were a key faction in the party, especially in San Francisco. Gays were also part of the radical "rights coalition," which included feminists and pro-abortion crusaders. The Democratic Party lined up behind the radicals and supported their efforts to block the enforcement of public health policy.

I interviewed Dr. Mervyn Silverman, the liberal director of public health for the City of San Francisco, and asked him why he didn't close the bathhouses, since they were greenhouses of the disease. He told me he wouldn't do so because they were valuable centers of "education" about AIDS.[17] He told me this even though there was no such education going on in them. The bathhouses existed only to facilitate anonymous, promiscuous, and dangerous public sex. I knew exactly where Dr. Silverman got his medical expertise on this subject. He was speaking the party line of the Sex Panic! fanatics.[18]

In fact, the public health system had long been developing and using successful methods for fighting sexually transmitted diseases. Testing and contact tracing were among the most tried and true measures to identify carriers and warn potential targets. Separating carriers from the uninfected who were at risk was the key to fighting an epidemic, as Don Francis had informed me.

But gay leaders successfully attacked and blocked both procedures, which would have made these precautions possible. They condemned commonsense preventive measures as "homophobic" efforts to stigmatize gays and identify them for future "roundups." Employing these proven public health measures, gay radicals claimed, would make the victims responsible for their plight. Such emotional arguments ignored the fact that those already victimized by AIDS were now potential predators able to infect healthy members of the gay community.

Studies showed that the sexual transmission of the virus overwhelmingly occurred through passive anal sex. Yet that term, or "promiscuous anal sex," never appeared in public health warnings about the disease—omissions demanded by gay leaders. A $100 million government "information" campaign, led by Surgeon General Everett Koop, was conducted with the slogan "AIDS is an equal opportunity virus." This claim—and only this claim—was politically permissible, according to gay leaders.

But the claim was false. Sexually transmitted AIDS wasn't an equal opportunity virus that affected heterosexuals and homosexuals alike. Twenty years into the epidemic, eight out of ten sexually transmitted AIDS cases stemmed from men having sex with men.[19]

A Preventable Death Toll

The only purpose of the "AIDS information" campaign was to soothe gay sensibilities, so gay people wouldn't fear that they were about to be put into concentration camps, as their leaders claimed. When public health officials tried to institute screening procedures for the nation's blood banks, and when they asked the gay community not to donate blood during the epidemic crisis, gay leaders denounced the proposals. They claimed that such proposals stigmatized homosexuals and infringed on their "right" to give blood.

The San Francisco Coordinating Committee of Gay and Lesbian Services, chaired by city official Pat Norman, issued a policy paper asserting that donor screening was "reminiscent of miscegenation blood laws that divided black blood from white" and "similar in concept to the World War II rounding up of Japanese-Americans in the western half of the country to minimize the possibility of espionage."[20] The fact that tainted blood donations gave surgical patients and other blood recipients a deadly incurable disease was not a consideration.

During my interview with Don Francis, I asked him when the primary public health methods of testing and contact tracing would be resumed. He said, "When enough people are dead." It never happened. Apparently, the death toll was never high enough. In 1983, when our AIDS story was published, there were only 3,000 AIDS cases nationally, but they were doubling every six months.[21]

When I was researching the AIDS article in 1983, many doctors and researchers I spoke to speculated—correctly, as it turned out—that an AIDS vaccine would be decades away, if one was ever developed at all. To date, there is no licensed HIV/AIDS vaccine, although HIV-infected patients are living longer thanks to new antiviral therapies. Hearing that prospects for a vaccine were so bleak made me feel helpless and deeply saddened. When I did a mental calculation of the coming death toll, I figured that in twenty years there would be 200,000 dead. My arithmetic was faulty. By 2003 there were 523,442 recorded deaths from AIDS in the United States, most of them young, and previously healthy, gay men.[22] Most of those deaths could have been prevented if the public health system had not been crippled by radical ideologues.

Attack on a Church

The gay radicals kept the bathhouses open as "symbols of the revolution." They shut down the testing and contact-tracing programs, which would have exposed the path of the epidemic, allowing health officials to warn those in its path. The radicals did, however, agree on one prophylactic measure to save lives: the use of condoms to practice "safe sex." The gay community leaders turned it into a campaign with posters proclaiming "Safe Sex Is Hot Sex."[23] Unlike other measures to prevent the spread of disease, condom use was not viewed as "homophobic" by the gay community and wouldn't interfere with the liberated lifestyle.

Using condoms was prudent advice, but it relied on the responsible behavior of individuals. Responsibility, on the other hand, was precisely the moral characteristic that gay liberation had thrown to the winds. Condom use also brought the activists up against the moral positions of their Christian nemesis, the Catholic Church. The church advocated sexual abstinence and opposed prophylactic measures, even though condoms didn't serve a contraceptive purpose in gay sex. In a statement titled, "Call to Compassion," the Catholic bishops warned against the notion of safe sex because it "compromises human sexuality and can lead to promiscuous behavior." Promiscuous behavior was, of course, the rallying cry of the liberationists—and the root cause of the epidemic.[24]

This moral conflict led directly to the most notorious demonstration of the AIDS-era protests. In 1989, Larry Kramer's newly formed ACT-UP (AIDS Coalition to Unleash Power) joined with WHAM! (Women's Health Action and Mobilization) to attack a Sunday mass at St. Patrick's Cathedral in New York City. Over 4,000 raucous protesters gathered outside the cathedral while dozens rushed inside screaming "You're killing us!" and "Murderers!" at the bewildered congregation. In a calculated outrage that brought widespread condemnation, even from the gay community, one activist crushed a wafer symbolizing the body of Christ. The cardinal called it a "desecration."

While extreme, these acts of violent hatred were not unusual. A *New York Times* reporter sympathetic to the gay cause observed:

Rarely are Act-Up's adversaries seen as well-meaning people working in a complicated world. In Act-Up's eyes they are liars, hypocrites—even murderers. In 1988, Dr. Joseph, then the city's Health Commissioner, reduced by half his estimate of the number of city residents infected by the virus. While Dr. Joseph accompanied his study with the warning that no one should think it "in any way reduces the services needed," Act-Up members accused him of a plot to accomplish that and other nefarious ends. They splashed paint and posters on his house, occupied his office, and called him a Nazi.[25]

Yet the *Times* story praised ACT-UP's offensive tactics for allegedly prodding the government to approve experimental drugs faster. Drugs, however, could not provide an immediate solution to the drug-resistant virus. Thirty years after the attack on St. Patrick's, medical advances have reduced fatalities and stemmed the tide of the epidemic—but there still is no cure for AIDS.

By promoting sexual promiscuity as a revolutionary act, by disregarding proven social restraints, and by viciously attacking all critics, gay activists led their own community into one of the worst human disasters in American history. The radicals were so focused on their agendas, and so bent on destroying their perceived enemies, that they lost sight of reality: their revolution was killing the people it was intended to liberate.

A Leftist Assault on Freedom and Equality

The radicals rejected the traditional American framework of pluralism, civility, and compromise in favor of a revolutionary agenda. Like radical feminists, they perceived any limits to their desires as oppression by the social order—concluding that the social order had to be destroyed. Such sweeping attempts at social transformation have brought disaster throughout history, no more so than in the last century, which saw epic catastrophes created by National Socialists and Communists seeking better worlds.

Unfortunately, the radical left was able to continue on its long march through America's institutions, particularly universities, the media culture, and the Democratic Party, coalescing its forces and marshaling its weapons under the ideological banner of "identity politics." This was the same politics that made the gay community resistant to proven public health methods and common sense. This was the same victim-versus-oppressor politics that caused homosexuals to view heterosexuals and "heteronormativity" as their enemies.

Since the seventies, the radical movement had been establishing a political base in the universities, purging conservative faculty and texts, and transforming scholarly disciplines into political training programs. These leftist indoctrination programs are referred to as "oppression studies," "social justice studies," "feminist studies," "whiteness studies," and the like. So advanced has this transformation become that Andrew Sullivan, a principled liberal and prominent gay activist, felt impelled to sound an alarm. He pointed out that this radical movement posed an existential threat to the American order of pluralism and individual freedom:

> When elite universities shift their entire worldview away from liberal education, as we have long known it, toward the imperatives of an identity-based "social justice" movement, the broader culture is in danger of drifting away from liberal democracy as well. If elites believe that the core truth of our society is a system of interlocking and oppressive power structures based around immutable characteristics like race or sex

or sexual orientation, then sooner rather than later, this will be reflected in our culture at large. What matters most of all in these colleges—your membership in a group that is embedded in a hierarchy of oppression—will soon enough be what matters in the society as a whole.[26]

Sullivan went on to describe how this notion constituted an assault on the fundamental American principle of the freedom and equality of individuals:

The whole concept of an individual who exists apart from group identity is slipping from the discourse. The idea of individual merit—as opposed to various forms of unearned "privilege"—is increasingly suspect. The Enlightenment principles that formed the bedrock of the American experiment—untrammeled free speech, due process, individual (rather than group) rights—are now routinely understood as mere masks for "white male" power, code words for the oppression of women and nonwhites. Any differences in outcome for various groups must always be a function of "hate," rather than a function of nature or choice or freedom or individual agency. And anyone who questions these assertions is obviously a white supremacist himself.

The only thing Sullivan missed in this ominous warning was the religious foundation of the principles under attack—the "priesthood of all believers" and the salvation of individual souls. These were the beliefs, rooted in faith, that made the Christian right the most vocal and dedicated opponent of the movement Sullivan feared.

10

Obama's Arc

WHEN BARACK OBAMA ENTERED the White House in January 2008, one of his first priorities was to install a new carpet in the Oval Office with this inscription: "The arc of the moral universe is long, but it bends toward justice." This is the religious premise of radical politics. It is why leftists identify their opponents as being "on the wrong side of history," and therefore against justice, since that is where history is allegedly heading. People who are against justice are obviously criminals. Radicals, by contrast, are on the "right side" of history because that is their mission: "social justice"—the creation of a humane world, such as has never existed before. This mission is so grandiose and such a noble act of social redemption as to sanction virtually any means to achieve it, while inspiring hatred for those who oppose it.

The Greeks were wiser, and humbler. They didn't believe in an inexorable, inevitable arc of history. They saw that civilizations rose and fell, and nothing lasts forever. This is also the conservative view as expressed in these famous words of Ronald Reagan: "Freedom is never more than one generation away from extinction. We didn't pass it to our children in the bloodstream. It must be fought for, protected, and handed on for them to do the same."[1] It is also the Christian view: The post-Edenic world is a fallen place, irreparably damaged by the corruption of human hearts, so that no human agency can heal it.

A Global Apology Tour

Barack Obama was raised by Communists and spent his entire life on the radical left before the Senate race that launched his national career. He was trained and employed by the network created by Saul Alinsky, the author of *Rules for Radicals*. In the dedication of this famous book, Alinsky paid tribute to "the first radical known to man who rebelled against the establishment and did it so effectively that he at least won his own kingdom—Lucifer."[2] Obama's family counselor, political advisor, and pastor for twenty years was the anti-American racist, Jeremiah Wright, who invoked God's damnation on America and who blamed America for bringing the 9/11 attacks upon itself. Obama's political collaborator and close friend was the unrepentant New Left terrorist William Ayers. Ayers personally took part in bombings of the

NewYorkCityPoliceDepartmentheadquarters,theCapitol Building, and the Pentagon in the early 1970s.

Obama was so steeped in his radical vision of a transformedAmericathathemadeittheclimaxofhisspeechwhen accepting the nomination of his party on June 3, 2008: "I am absolutely certain that generations from now, we will be able to look back and tell our children that this was the moment when we began to provide care for the sick and good jobs to the jobless; this was the moment when the rise of the oceans began to slow and our planet began to heal."[3] He repeated this extravagant ambition on the eve of the November election, proclaiming, "We are five days away from fundamentally transforming the United States of America."[4]

Obama's radicalism led to a call to arms among conservatives, and conservative Christians in particular. Ben Carson, a presidential primary candidate in 2016, recalled the homage that Obama's role model, Alinsky, had paid to the "first rebel," Lucifer: "[Alinsky] wrote a book called *Rules for Radicals*. On the dedication page it acknowledges Lucifer, the original radical 'who gained his own kingdom.' Now think about that. This is a nation where our founding document, the Declaration of Independence, talks about certain inalienable rights that come from our creator, a nation where our Pledge of Alliance says we are 'One nation under God.'"[5]

Religious Americans had already felt the sting of Obama's contempt during the presidential campaign. Referring to working-class voters in the Midwest who were angry over trade policies that had caused their jobs to disappear, he said, "They get bitter, they cling to guns or religion or antipathy to people who aren't like them or anti-immigrant sentiment or anti-trade sentiment as a way to explain their frustrations."[6] The clear meaning of these words was that religious people and other victims of bad economic policies who turned to conservative politics to redress their grievances were racists, anti-immigrants, and haters of "people who aren't like them." This was a veritable litany of the attacks that were the common themes of the Democratic Party over Obama's eight years in office—and beyond.

President Obama began his administration with an unprecedented "apology tour" of foreign capitals, humiliating his own country in front of over 3 billion citizens of foreign nations. He began his tour in Cairo, an Islamic capital, where he apologized for America's alleged sins, even though thousands of Americans had been murdered in 9/11 and other attacks by Islamic terrorists with little protest from Islamic governments. He apologized to Europeans and to Cuban Communists, expressing regret over American policies that had allegedly led to their differences with, and antagonisms toward, the United States.

A Heritage Foundation report, "Barack Obama's Top 10 Apologies: How the President Has Humiliated a Superpower," concluded, "A common theme that runs through President Obama's statements is the idea the United States must atone for its past policies, whether it is America's application of the war against Islamist terrorism or its overall foreign policy."[7]

Steps Toward Revival

The contrast between Obama's view of America and that of the religious right and conservatives in general could not have been greater. To celebrate the bicentennial of the Declaration of Independence on July 4, 1976, Jerry Falwell had organized a rally on Liberty Mountain, the campus of his Liberty Baptist College. At the rally, 25,000 Christians assembled to sing hymns and patriotic songs. The event featured a sermon by Falwell's fundamentalist mentor, B. R. Lakin, foretelling the Great Awakening that was coming to American politics.

Falwell also held 112 "I Love America" rallies across the country. Their purpose was to revive patriotic feeling and religious faith. These would become central themes of the Moral Majority, the organization he founded in 1979 to take those values into the political arena. Each rally began with a rendering of "Faith of Our Fathers" and "America the Beautiful."

The biblical theme for the rallies was II Chronicles 7:14: "If my people, which are called by my name, shall humble themselves, and pray, and seek my face, and turn from their wicked ways, then will I hear from heaven, and forgive their sin, and will heal the land." This Old Testament passage, observed a Falwell biographer, "summarized what Falwell was after: genuine national religious repentance followed by assertive steps towards national revival."[8]

Standing in the way of such a revival were the anti-American attitudes of the political left, now instantiated in the White House of Barack Obama. A centerpiece of Obama's foreign policy was the effort to diminish America's role in the world. Among his first acts was to formally end America's "war on terror." According to every reputable survey, hundreds of millions of Muslims supported those attacks, and tens of thousands of "infidels" had already died at the hands of Islamic terrorists. Yet President Obama denied that Islam had anything to do with these facts.

Two months into his administration, the commander-in-chief ordered the term "war on terror" dropped from official U.S. policy manuals and statements. The new term would be "Overseas Contingency Operations"—a bland bureaucratic descriptor under which to file America's ongoing response to terror attacks.[9]

Three months later, in June 2009, tens of thousands of Iranian protesters filled the streets of Teheran, hoping to overthrow the terrorist regime of the Iranian mullahs. Iran had killed thousands of Americans in Lebanon and Iraq. Its national slogans were "Death to America" and "Death to Israel." Despite the declared enmity of the regime, Obama gave no support—verbal or practical—to the protestors, even as they were being arrested and shot by Iran's Revolutionary Guards.

The reason for President Obama's hands-off policy toward the Iranian protests was only disclosed years later. The reason was that he was planning to end the Iranian regime's international isolation, lift its economic sanctions, and transfer billions of dollars to its treasury. His goal was a deal that would provide Iran's terrorist rulers with a path to nuclear weapons without requiring any changes in the regime's behavior.[10]

Obama's cold indifference toward the Iranian dissidents and their government oppressors contrasted sharply with his interventionist approach to an American ally, Hosni Mubarak, the president of Egypt. Mubarak was the leader of the most important Arab nation in the Middle East. In the name of "human rights"—a value that didn't seem to inform Obama's attitude toward Syria or Iran—he pressured Mubarak to step down and hailed the protesters against Mubarak's autocratic rule as an "inspiration."

The fall of the Mubarak regime paved the way for the ascension of the Muslim Brotherhood, the only major organized political force in Egypt at the time. The Brotherhood, which was the fountainhead of al-Qaeda and Sunni Islamic terrorism generally, was overthrown the following year by the Egyptian military and General Abdel Fattah el-Sisi, on whom Obama immediately turned his back. The effect of Obama's cold shoulder was to invite Russia's intrusion into the Middle East. By diminishing America's influence in the Middle East, President Obama presided over the end of Washington's role as the dominant outside power in the region. This in turn led to a Russian-Syrian-Iranian alliance prosecuting the Syrian civil war.

This was hardly a complete list of Obama's retreats. In Iraq, he failed to insist on a "status of forces" agreement that would have left 20,000 American troops in place. He also failed to retain control of America's giant military base in Baghdad. Secretary of Defense Leon Panetta, Under Secretary of Defense Michèle Flournoy, Deputy Secretary of Defense Ash Carter, military commanders in the region, and the Joint Chiefs of Staff had pleaded with Obama to insist on a continued troop presence and the retention of America's military base.

Secretary of Defense Panetta had warned Obama that if Iraq "split apart or slid back into the violence that we'd seen in the years immediately following the U.S. invasion, it could become a new haven for terrorists to plot attacks against the U.S. Iraq's stability was not only in Iraq's interest but also in ours." It soon became apparent to Panetta and his aides that the Obama White House was "so eager to rid itself of Iraq that it was willing to withdraw rather than lock in arrangements that would preserve our influence and interests."[11]

These withdrawals betrayed all the American and Iraqi troops who had given their lives to keep that country from falling into the hands of Iran and the terrorists. It was also a betrayal of American taxpayers, who had invested a trillion dollars in the war effort. The power vacuum this withdrawal created led directly to the resurgence of al-Qaeda and the rise of the Islamic State (ISIS), the most barbarous Islamic terrorist army yet.

The first priority of ISIS was the genocide of the oldest Christian community in the world. While Obama said little and had America's military mainly stand by, ISIS proceeded to slaughter hundreds of thousands of Christians and drive the survivors into exile. America's Christians could not help but be horrified by Obama's double standards when it came to their religion and Islam's.

Faced with rising concern over Islamist terrorism, which had murdered over 30,000 "infidels" since 9/11, Obama responded by lecturing Americans on alleged crimes Christians had committed 800 years earlier during the Crusades, and their alleged guilt for American slavery and Jim Crow laws in the South. Speaking at the National Prayer Breakfast on February 5, 2015, President Obama said, "And lest we get on our high horse and think this is unique to some other place, remember that during the Crusades and the Inquisition, people committed terrible deeds in the name of Christ. In our home country, slavery and Jim Crow all too often was justified in the name of Christ."[12]

The Crusades were not a criminal enterprise like Islamic terrorism, but an attempt to liberate the Christian Holy Land from its Muslim conquerors. By the time the Crusades were initiated by Pope Urban II in the early eleventh century, roughly half of all Christian lands were occupied by Muslim conquerors. Cities where the Christian church once flourished—Jerusalem (Christianity's birthplace), Antioch, Damascus, Carthage, Alexandria—had all been conquered by the sword in the name of Allah and the Prophet. Crusaders did sometimes commit atrocities They were not fighting a war of aggression like the Islamic jihad, however, but a defensive war against Islamic conquest.

Contrary to Obama's perverse view of American history, Christian America led the world in ending slavery, beginning with the Declaration of Independence's proclamation that all mankind had a God-given unalienable right to liberty. Prominent Christian abolitionists included evangelical revivalist Charles Finney, evangelical minister Lyman Beecher (father of Harriet Beecher Stowe, the author of *Uncle Tom's Cabin*), the devoutly Christian escaped slave Sojourner Truth, and the many Quaker abolitionists of the eighteenth and nineteenth centuries. Christian America fought a civil war to abolish slavery once and for all, while slavery is still practiced in Muslim Africa.

Segregation was outlawed by the Civil Rights Acts fifty years before Barack Obama lectured Christians on the sins of the Jim Crow era. The man who led the civil rights crusade was a courageous Protestant minister, Dr. Martin Luther King, Jr.

Under Obama's patronage, the anti-God, antireligious left steadily tightened its grip on the Democratic Party. One index of its success was the removal of the word "God" from its official platform. The 2004 Democratic platform had affirmed the Democrats' dedication to "faith and family, duty and service, individual freedom and a common purpose to build one nation under God." By 2012 no reference to God appeared in the Democratic platform.

During the platform debate that year, former Ohio governor Ted Strickland, mindful of the religious sentiments of his constituents, proposed to insert a reference to "God-given potential" and also to restore the promise Obama had made (and not kept) to recognize Jerusalem as the capital of Israel. Official recognition of Jerusalem as Israel's capital was a cause that was near to the heart of the Christian right. The platform committee, however, removed Strickland's items.

Restoring them would require an amendment. Knowing that the amendment might fail, convention chair Antonio Villaraigosa attempted to pass the amendment by a voice vote. But it failed three times. After the third failure, Villaraigosa ruled that the amendment had actually passed, whereupon the hall erupted with Democratic delegates jeering and booing. "Democrats boo God" became the headline of the day.

The booing was a sign of how far the Democrats had slid into the embrace of the antireligious, anti-American left; and how they had turned religious faith into a partisan division between Democrats and Republicans, between left and right.

11

Religious Liberty

BRIGADIER GENERAL E. JOHN Teichert commands the 412th Test Wing, Edwards Air Force Base, California. He is responsible for the second largest base in the Air Force—and he's under attack because he maintains a website called "Prayer at Lunchtime for the United States." On the site, he identifies himself only as "John." He doesn't speak for the Air Force—only himself. The website encourages Christians to "pray for our nation at lunchtime every day." He suggests that people pray for the president and vice president, the Congress, and the military. He also asks prayer for "the unborn" and for "a return to our biblical foundation."

Michael Weinstein, founder of the Military Religious Freedom Foundation, claims the general's prayer website is "unconstitutional." Weinstein describes General Teichert as a "fundamentalist Christian tyrant and religious extremist predator" who promotes a "weaponized version of Christianity."[1]

Weinstein's Military Religious Freedom Foundation is not a religious liberty advocacy group, but an extreme anti-Christian hate group. Its deceptive mission statement focuses only on the Establishment Clause of the First Amendment and ignores the Free Exercise Clause which guarantees Americans like General Teichert the right to express their religious views freely. Using the banner of religious freedom to suppress religious freedom is perfectly Orwellian and is what totalitarians do.

A month after Obama's inauguration, the *New York Times* reported that a meeting between Weinstein and Air Force General Norton A. Schwartz was "the first time the group has gotten an audience with a member of the Joint Chiefs of Staff."[2] As a result of Weinstein's subsequent influence with the Pentagon, during the Obama years, religious expression in the military became a criminal offense. Weinstein made the case to the Pentagon that Christians in the military—including chaplains—who shared their beliefs with others were committing "treason" and "spiritual rape." He called service personnel who openly talked about their faith "enemies of the Constitution."

Under President Obama and Secretary of Defense Chuck Hagel, the Pentagon adopted Weinstein's false view that the First Amendment was an antireligious stricture. In 2013, the Pentagon released a statement warning that soldiers would not be permitted to talk openly about their faith. "Religious proselytization is not permitted within the Department of Defense," the statement said. The Pentagon statement also noted ominously, "Court martials and non-judicial punishments are decided on a case-by-case basis."

This warning was issued after *Breitbart News* reported that Obama appointees in the Pentagon were meeting with Weinstein and the Military Religious Freedom Foundation to develop court-martial protocols to deal with Christians in uniform who shared their faith with others.[3] The punishment meted out by a court-martial may include imprisonment and a dishonorable discharge.

An op-ed Weinstein wrote for the *Huffington Post* illustrates his ignorant extremism, which he has dedicated to the suppression of religious liberty in the military. "I founded the civil rights fighting organization the Military Religious Freedom Foundation to do one thing: fight those monsters who would tear down the Constitutionally-mandated wall separating church and state in the technologically most lethal entity ever created by humankind, the U.S. military." Weinstein identified his opponents as "incredibly well-funded gangs of fundamentalist Christian monsters who terrorize their fellow Americans by forcing their weaponized and twisted version of Christianity upon their helpless subordinates in our nation's armed forces."

He went on: "Evil, fundamentalist Christian creatures and their spiritual heirs have taken refuge behind flimsy, well-worn, gauze-like euphemistic facades such as 'family values' and 'religious liberty.'" Christians "coagulate their stenchful substances" in such organizations as the American Family Association, the "ultra-fundamentalist" Family Research

Council, and Chaplains Alliance for Religious Liberty. Weinstein concluded with a warning that his readers need to speak out against the "fundamentalist Christian monsters of human degradation, marginalization, humiliation and tyranny" lest they one day find themselves living under a "rapacious reign of theocratic terror."[4]

The fact that the Obama Pentagon would even consult with the unhinged author of such rabid sentiments, let alone institutionalize his antireligious attitudes, is an ominous indication of what the future may hold if radicals like Weinstein continue to have their day.

Fundamentally Transforming America

Religious liberty is America's first freedom and the foundation of all American freedoms. It's the reason America's settlers and founders came to these shores and why they set up America's system of unalienable rights. Freedom of conscience, derived from "the priesthood of all believers," is the cornerstone of American pluralism, making possible the diversity of America's communities, their equality under the law, and their ability to peacefully coexist.

The left's attacks on religious freedom, and general hatred for those who don't agree with them, are driven by "identity politics." Identity politics is an anti-American ideology and a sanitized name for cultural Marxism. Marx viewed market societies as divided into capitalists and workers, to which he ascribed moral attributes: oppressors and oppressed. Society was the site of continual warfare between these classes. Cultural Marxists have extended this picture of class warfare to races, genders, and sexual orientations, attributing all inequality and injustice to the institutions and actions of the oppressor groups: whites, males, heterosexuals, and religious "reactionaries"—in particular Christians—whose views allegedly serve the interests of the oppressors.

Contrary to Marx and the identity politics left, which now includes the Democratic Party, the source of inequalities between individuals is not the work of oppressor groups, but is a combination of circumstance (often beyond one's control), individual talents, and choice. As Christians, the American founders believed in free will—the responsibility of individuals for their actions and the results of those actions. Free will is what makes us equal, so long as government does not restrict our freedom. Recognizing that individuals make choices, which affect their destinies, puts the responsibility for overcoming the handicaps of circumstance squarely on the individual's shoulders. This is a liberating idea. It is why America's inspirational stories are always stories about the triumph of the underdog, the ability of individuals to overcome their circumstances, to rise above their allotted stations in life, to achieve something better. For over 200 years that vision has been the American dream.

Until now. Identity politics—which is currently the politics of the Democratic Party—rejects this inspirational idea and attributes inequality to the machinations of oppressor groups, who are defined by race, gender, and sexual orientation, characteristics that an individual cannot change. This is a prescription for true oppression, as the government steps in to create "social justice" by depriving those who have earned it, the fruits of their labor, and distributing them to those who have not. It is a prescription for irreconcilable conflict and division, not the compromise and coexistence that the American founders worked so hard to achieve. The success of the cultural Marxists in reshaping our institutions is why America now appears to be two nations instead of one.

If the source of inequality is not circumstance, individual talent, and choice, but is imposed by an oppressor group, it can only be overcome by suppressing that group. It is therefore morally wrong to extend sympathy to an oppressor group or to respect its American rights—rights once afforded to all. To respect oppressors' rights is to support the injustices they commit. If social justice is to be achieved, one must suppress the perpetrators of injustice by depriving them of their rights. That is why progressives—cultural Marxists—are so intolerant and seek to suppress the free speech of those who oppose them.

In identity politics only collective rights matter—not individual rights. What matters is one's membership in a "victim" group or an "oppressor" group. Membership is based on characteristics the individual cannot change. Identity politics is a politics of hate, and a prescription for war. The liberal but anti-left writer Andrew Sullivan has eloquently summed up the consequences of this view of the world:

> What matters [to the left] is that nonwhites fight and defeat white supremacy, that women unite and defeat oppressive masculinity, and that the trans [gendered] supplant and redefine the cis [people whose sense of their own identity corresponds to their birth sex]. What matters is equality of outcome, and it cannot be delayed. All the ideas that might

complicate this—meritocracy, for example, or a color-blind vision of justice, or equality of opportunity rather than out-come—are to be mocked until they are dismantled. And the political goal is not a post-racial fusion, a unity of the red and the blue, but the rallying of the victims against the vic-timizers, animated by the core belief that a non-"white" and non-male majority will at some point come, after which the new hierarchies can be imposed by fiat.[5]

In other words, by a totalitarian state.

Barack Obama's effort to "fundamentally transform the United States of America" began with a major legislative ini-tiative, misnamed the "Affordable Care Act," better known as Obamacare. This massive government program was first of all an assault on individual freedom, taking away the right to choose one's doctor and healthcare plan. In order to sell the plan to the public, Obama had to deliberately lie and say, "If you like your doctor, you can keep your doctor. Period." He spoke this lie again and again, using ironclad-sounding lan-guage like "promise," "pledge," and "guarantee" to socialize America's healthcare system.

Because the plan was a frontal assault on the American sys-tem of individual accountability and freedom, the lies were central to getting Obamacare passed. They were even used to deceive the Congressional Budget Office and the Democrats in Congress who voted for it. In an unguarded videotaped moment during a panel discussion at the University of Pennsylvania, Jonathan Gruber, a chief architect of the plan, revealed the reasoning behind the lies:

This bill was written in a tortured way to make sure [the Congressional Budget Office] did not score the mandate as taxes. If CBO scored the mandate as taxes, the bill dies, okay? ... If you made it explicit that healthy people pay in and sick people get money, it would not have passed, okay? Lack of transparency is a huge political advantage. And basically, you know, call it the stupidity of the American voter or whatever. But basically, that was really, really critical to getting the thing to pass.[6]

This is the way authoritarian governments think and act. It is the opposite of what was once the American way.

Big Government Versus the Little Sisters

Obamacare also provided its bureaucratic social engineers with the power to invent—without consent of Congress— additional mandates to impose on the public. One of these was an anti-conscience requirement that employers must provide insurance coverage for abortion-inducing drugs, contraceptives, and sterilization, even if such provisions violated the employer's religious convictions.[7]

Because religious liberty is the foundation of all liberties, the ramifications of the Obama policy went far beyond an assault on religious institutions. It was a dagger aimed at the heart of the First Amendment—and the ability of the American people to form their own communities of belief.

"What is at stake here ultimately," explained the Catholic scholar George Weigel, "is whether civil society will survive, and whether voluntary institutions or voluntary associations ranging from the traditional family to multimillion member organizations like the Catholic Church to small businesses will be allowed to function only if they imitate the government, only if they imitate the state." In other words, what was at stake was whether America would remain a democracy or move in the direction of a totalitarian state.

"What is happening," agreed the Heritage Foundation's Matthew Spalding, "has little to do with health care or even public policy and everything to do with the role of government in the most immediate and intimate matters of our lives." Under Obamacare, "all is subject to government control, regulatory dictate, and administrative whim. Nothing will be allowed outside of the new regulatory scheme: no independent state programs, no individuals or businesses permitted not to participate, no true private market alternatives."[8]

The brutal, anti-American implications of the Obamacare mandates were made immediately clear in the government's assault on a religious charity called the Little Sisters of the Poor.

Founded in France in 1839 by Saint Jeanne Jugan, Little Sisters of the Poor was originally a religious institute for women. Saint Jeanne would travel the streets of French towns with her begging baskets, seeking alms to care for the elderly poor. Today, members make vows of chastity, poverty, obedience, and hospitality. They serve the poor in thirty-one countries including the United States. "Our vision," explains the official website, "is to contribute to the Culture of Life by nurturing communities where each person is valued, the solidarity of the human family and the wisdom of age are celebrated, and the compassionate love of Christ is shared with all."

As a Catholic organization, the Little Sisters could not comply with the Obamacare mandate to provide abortion-inducing drugs and contraceptives to the elderly women they served. Failure to comply, however, meant millions of dollars in fines. This forced the Little Sisters to go to court to defend themselves.[9]

Because the Little Sisters were themselves celibate and served elderly women, the Obama administration's position was obviously ludicrous. It was vindictive from the outset. But even when their motives were exposed, Obama's agents refused to relent. Imposing their views on others was so important to the radicals, as the essence of the plan to fundamentally transform America, that they forced the Little Sisters to undergo years of costly legal battles to defend the religious freedom that is plainly guaranteed by the First Amendment.

A nun representing the sisters explained, "The government basically forced us into a corner. We have no desire to litigate against our government, but we had no choice because we cannot participate in the moral evil of providing or facilitating the provision of abortion and contraception."[10] She also explained why the Little Sisters felt conscience-bound to take a principled stand against the mandate, even though neither the sisters nor their elderly clients would ever need contraceptives or abortions: "As Little Sisters of the Poor we vow to devote our lives specifically to the service of the elderly poor, but the unborn are no less worthy of reverence and protection than the frail seniors we serve every day."[11]

As the appeals progressed through the courts, the nuns' belief in the "sanctity of life" was attacked by feminists as unconstitutional discrimination against women. The Little Sisters were putting an "undue burden" on women and were therefore part of the oppressor class.

In a case that should have been open-and-shut on First Amendment grounds (the free exercise of religion), the sisters were forced onto the legal treadmill in 2013. Their appeals were repeatedly rejected through 2015, when the Tenth Circuit Court of Appeals ruled against them. It wasn't until 2016, when the case reached the Supreme Court, that the Little Sisters finally won their First Amendment religious liberty. By a unanimous vote the justices struck down the Obama administration's case, so weak were its legal foundations.

What was striking about this case, and typical of many similar ones, was its vindictive nature—the willingness of Obama bureaucrats to pursue the indefensible: to prosecute individuals who were clearly sincere in their religious convictions and seeking the protection of the most fundamental liberty that Americans enjoy.

The spectacle of a Big Government bureaucracy bullying the Little Sisters of the Poor seemed like a story scripted for a Hallmark Channel movie. Yet the Obama administration didn't care how it looked—and was probably confident that the Hallmark Channel would not provide a platform for a story that exposed what the administration had done. Under the cloak of "social justice," the government radicals were determined to prove that their mandates must be obeyed. Not even the First Amendment could be allowed to stand in the way of fundamentally transforming America.

A "Constitutional Right" Not Found in the Constitution

For eight years, the Obama administration was relentless in casting religious institutions and individuals as bigots and seeking to stifle religious voices. A faith-based website chronicled scores of incidents that exemplify the Obama administration's war on Christian America. The website identified Barack Obama as "America's Most Biblically Hostile U.S. President."[12] The list reads in part:

ACTS OF HOSTILITY TOWARD PEOPLE OF BIBLICAL FAITH

December 2009–Present—The annual White House Christmas cards, rather than focusing on Christmas or faith, instead highlight things such as the family dogs. And the White House Christmas tree ornaments which include figures such as Mao Tse-Tung and a drag queen.

March 2009—The Obama administration shut out pro-life groups from attending a White House-sponsored health care summit.

April 2009—In a deliberate act of disrespect, Obama nominated three pro-abortion ambassadors to the Vatican; of course, the pro-life Vatican rejected all three.

April 2009—When speaking at Georgetown University, Obama orders that a monogram symbolizing Jesus' name be covered when he is making his speech.

September 16, 2009—The Obama administration appoints as EEOC Commissioner Chai Feldblum, who asserts that society should "not tolerate" any "private beliefs," including religious beliefs, if they may negatively affect homosexual "equality."

May 2009—The White House budget eliminates all funding for abstinence-only education and replaces it with "comprehensive" sexual education, repeatedly proven to increase teen pregnancies and abortions. He continues the deletion in subsequent budgets.

May 2009—Obama officials assemble a terrorism dictionary calling pro-life advocates violent and charging that they use racism in their "criminal" activities.

May 2009—Obama declines to host services for the National Day of Prayer (a day established by federal law) at the White House.

July 2009—The Obama administration illegally extends federal benefits to same-sex partners of Foreign Service and Executive Branch employees, in direction violation of the federal Defense of Marriage Act.

October 19, 2010—Obama begins deliberately omitting the phrase about "the Creator" when quoting the Declaration of Independence—an omission he has made on no less than seven occasions.

August 2010—The Obama administration cuts funding for 176 abstinence education programs.

January 2011—After a federal law was passed to transfer a WWI Memorial in the Mojave Desert to private ownership, the U. S. Supreme Court ruled that the cross in the memorial could continue to stand, but the Obama administration refused to allow the land to be transferred as required by law, and refused to allow the cross to be re-erected as ordered by the Court.

February 2011—Although he filled posts in the State Department, for more than two years Obama did not fill the post of religious freedom ambassador, an official that works against religious persecution across the world.

April 2011—For the first time in American history, Obama urges passage of a non-discrimination law that does not contain hiring protections for religious groups, forcing religious organizations to hire according to federal mandates without regard to the dictates of their own faith, thus eliminating conscience protection in hiring.

November 2011—Unlike previous presidents, Obama studiously avoids any religious references in his Thanksgiving speech.

November 2011—President Obama opposes inclusion of President Franklin Roosevelt's famous D-Day Prayer in the WWII Memorial.

February 2012—The Obama administration forgives student loans in exchange for public service, but announces it will no longer forgive student loans if the public service is related to religion.

January 2013—Pastor Louie Giglio is pressured to remove himself from praying at the inauguration after it is discovered he once preached a sermon supporting the biblical definition of marriage.

March 2014—The Obama administration seeks funding for every type of sex-education—except that which reflects traditional moral values.

Ever the politician, Obama publicly opposed gay marriage well into his administration. But as the tide of public opinion began to change and made it safe for him to express his real views, he endorsed it and put his weight behind a series of cases that led to a June 2015 Supreme Court decision making same-sex marriage a constitutional right. There are many arguments for sanctioning gay unions, including the same religious considerations that regard families as indispensable foundations of decent societies. As the AIDS epidemic demonstrated, unattached males are dangerous to themselves and others. There are also different ways to legitimize same-sex couples and provide them with rights, such as civil unions.

In the normal democratic process, these questions would have been publicly debated and resolved with new legislation. The American people would, through their elected representatives, come to a consensus. In fact, by the time the Supreme

Court reached its decision, 60 percent of Americans, polled by the Gallup organization, already thought gay marriage should be law.[13]

Was it necessary for the radical left to again go over the heads of the people? Was it necessary to keep the American people from voicing their own views on how this issue should be resolved? Was it necessary to appeal again to nine unelected lawyers to assert a "constitutional right" not found in the Constitution?

There Would Be No Compromise

Using the Court to take a shortcut past the legislative process is an attack on the very heart of the American system. It deprives the people of a voice in their own government. The founders designed our representative democracy as a way to force diverse communities and factions to debate, to negotiate, and to reach compromises if possible. As legal scholar Lino Graglia observed, the decision demonstrated the arbitrary nature of the Court's power, the tyranny-in-the-making that its decision represented:

> Even for Americans unfortunately grown used to having radical cultural changes decreed by the Court, it should be impressive that the Court could by a margin of one vote decree that "marriage" no longer means the union of one man and one woman and deprive fifty state legislatures and Congress of the power to have it retain that meaning. At the same time, it could hardly be clearer that the decision, as Chief Justice Roberts pointed out in dissent, has nothing to do with the Constitution. It is an egregious example of

the Court's usurpation of legislative authority. To accept it without protest is in effect to accept a change in our form of government, from the system of representative self-government in a federalism with separation of powers created by the Constitution to government, to a large extent, by the Supreme Court.[14]

In making same-sex marriage a constitutional right, the Court not only bypassed the legislative process; it laid the groundwork for attacks by gay rights groups on the religious liberty of those they opposed. These were manifested in suits brought by LGBTQ individuals against businesspeople such as bakers, florists, nonprofits, and higher educational institutions with traditional views of marriage. One celebrated case highlighted the aggressiveness of the gay campaign and its destructive impacts on individuals in its path.

In 2012, a gay couple walked into a well-known Christian bakery in Colorado, the Masterpiece Cakeshop, in a deliberate attempt to provoke a confrontation. The owner was a soft-spoken individual named Jack Phillips. The gay couple demanded he bake them a wedding cake. Phillips told them he would bake them any cake in the store but not a wedding cake, because it would send a message endorsing gay weddings, which went against his religious principles. He said he could not go against his religious conscience to make them that particular cake, any more than he would make them a Halloween cake or a cake carrying an anti-American message.[15]

Even though Phillips manifested no ill will toward them as gays, on hearing his response the couple began cursing him and attacking his store. They then walked out to file a complaint with the Colorado Civil Rights Commission, claiming Phillips discriminated against gays, even though Phillips had been willing to serve them.

The commission ruled against Phillips, with one of the commissioners saying:

> Freedom of religion and religion have been used to justify all kinds of discrimination throughout history, whether it be slavery, whether it be the holocaust, whether it be—I mean, we can list hundreds of situations where freedom of religion has been used to justify discrimination. And to me it is one of the most despicable pieces of rhetoric that people can use, to use their religion to hurt others.[16]

When the case against Phillips reached the Supreme Court six years later, this outburst was deemed discriminatory itself and resulted in a decision against the plaintiffs.

In the six-year interim, Phillips had been barred from baking wedding cakes, which were 40 percent of his business. He was forced to pay $175,000 in legal fees to defend himself, while he and his family were subjected to constant verbal attacks. "We've had death threats," Phillips told ABC News. "We've had hundreds of phone calls and emails that were vile and vulgar and vicious."

One death threat was called in to his store while his daughter, who also worked at the bakery, and his granddaughter were present. The anonymous caller said he was coming to the shop to make good on his threat. Phillips recalled, "I had to have [my daughter and granddaughter] go hide in the back. It was a crazy situation."[17]

In each of these cases, the Obama administration was fully behind the gay vigilantes. As two writers for *National Review* observed, "The administration was content to depict any religious institution or person holding fast to traditional beliefs on marriage as engaging in invidious forms of discrimination." Other commentators pointed out, "Each of the dissenting justices [in the Supreme Court case on gay marriage] specifically highlighted the ways in which the ruling represented an enormous threat to religious liberty. But in the months following the Court's ruling, the administration made clear that there would be no compromise."[18]

Switching from Jefferson to Marx

An even more ominous aspect of the Court's ruling was the way the majority of justices embraced leftist identity politics and victimology. Meanwhile, the Court's majority completely ignored the threat the decision posed to the pluralistic principle at the heart of America's social contract.

Before making same-sex marriage a constitutional right, the Court had to void the 1996 Defense of Marriage Act, passed by Congress during the Clinton administration. The act had defined marriage, for federal purposes, as "only the legal union of one man and one woman as husband and wife."[19] It was overturned in the 2013 *United States v. Windsor* case, in which the same Court majority declared the Defense of Marriage Act discriminatory and unconstitutional. In a scathing dissent, Justice Scalia wrote:

> The majority says that the supporters of [the Defense of Marriage Act] acted with malice—with the "purpose to

disparage and to injure" same-sex couples. It says that the motivation for DOMA was to "demean," to "impose inequality," to "impose . . . a stigma," to deny people "equal dignity," to brand gay people as "unworthy," and to "humiliate" their children.

I am sure these accusations are quite untrue. To be sure (as the majority points out), the legislation is called the Defense of Marriage Act. But to defend traditional marriage is not to condemn, demean, or humiliate those who would prefer other arrangements, any more than to defend the Constitution of the United States is to condemn, demean, or humiliate other constitutions. To hurl such accusations so casually demeans this institution.

In the majority's judgment, any resistance to its holding is beyond the pale of reasoned disagreement. To question its high-handed invalidation of a presumptively valid statute is to act with the purpose to "disparage," "injure," "degrade," "demean," and "humiliate" our fellow human beings, our fellow citizens, who are homosexual. All that, simply for supporting an act that did no more than codify an aspect of marriage that had been unquestioned in our society for most of its existence—indeed, had been unquestioned in virtually all societies for virtually all of human history. It is one thing for a society to elect change; it is another for a court of law to impose change by adjudging those who oppose it *hostes humani generis*—enemies of the human race.[20]

Scalia had put the problem in a nutshell. There could hardly be a more precise description of the aggressions of a left that had switched its ideological allegiance from Jefferson to Marx, creating in the process the cavernous divisions in America's political life.

In July 2016, alarmed by the assaults on religious liberty and the Obama administration's disregard for freedom of conscience, congressional Republicans drew up a Conscience Protection Act. The act was designed to "protect health care providers that decline to be involved in abortions as a matter of conscience." Speaker Paul Ryan explained that the act was "meant to guard against exactly what [had already] happened in California, where all employers—including churches—are now required to cover abortions."[21]

On a straight party-line vote, the Conscience Protection Act was quickly passed in the Republican-dominated House. It was opposed by every Democrat on the grounds that it would "deny women full access to health care." Justifying the opposition, Colorado Democrat Diana DeGette assumed the victim posture and declared: "Congress needs to stop interfering in women's health decisions once and for all." The Obama White House claimed the act would "limit women's health care choices" and indicated that the president would probably issue a veto if it passed the Senate.[22]

At that moment, the Republican Party was holding its 2016 nominating convention in Cleveland, where its platform committee adopted a plank that read:

> Right of conscience is the first freedom to be protected. Religious freedom in the Bill of Rights protects the right of the people to practice their faith in their everyday lives. As George Washington taught, "religion and morality are indispensable supports" to a free society. Similarly, Thomas

Jefferson declared that "No provision in our Constitution ought to be dearer to man than that which protects the rights of conscience against the enterprises of the civil authority."[23]

When the First Amendment was adopted in 1791, the principle that Congress shall make no law prohibiting the free exercise of religion was plainly understood by every American, including lawmakers and judges. Today, the free exercise of religion has ceased to be a guaranteed right in America. Instead, it has become a battlefield.

12

Civil War

WITH THE VICTORY OF Donald Trump in the 2016 election, the nation's political divisions reached new levels of acrimony and distrust. Before the new president had settled into the Oval Office, congressional Democrats were boycotting his inauguration, calling for his impeachment, and declaring their opposition movement a "Resistance." The last time Democrats mounted a resistance to a duly elected president was in 1860, when the commander-in-chief was Abraham Lincoln. Commentators quickly began referring to the partisan conflicts that accompanied Trump's victory as America's "Second Civil War."

Observers on the left were bewildered by Trump's success, particularly his support from evangelicals and religious

Americans. According to Pew Research, 81 percent of evangelicals voted for Trump, a man who seemed anything but a model of Christian morality.[1] Evangelicals still voted for him—and it made leftists apoplectic. Typical of their reactions was a piece by *The Nation*'s Katha Pollitt, who fumed—in a typically deranged manner—that the only good thing to come from the "terrible, terrifying Trump years" was "the discrediting of evangelical Christianity.... They've sold their souls to Donald Trump, who has partaken freely of practically every vice and depravity known to man."[2] The left could not fathom why Christians preferred a morally flawed man, in Trump, who promised to defend religious liberty over a morally flawed woman, in Hillary, who was bound to take it away.

Not only did liberals attack Trump viciously, but they held *Trump* responsible for the unhinged nature of the attacks on him. To Trump's enemies, he provoked this bitterly personal warfare against him by his unorthodox, combative political style. They thought: What should Trump expect after tagging his opponent "Crooked Hillary"?

In fact, Trump is more accurately seen as a political *counter*puncher, and most of his barbs were reactions to others' attacks on him. Hillary and her proxies had already called him a racist and deplorable and not fit for office. His survival in the sixteen-candidate Republican primary had been a clinic in how to throw rivals off balance while responding to their challenges. At the same time, it's safe to say, no president in history has been the subject of as many, or as vicious, verbal assaults (including personal attacks on himself and his family) as Donald Trump.

Trump was a lightning rod for political divisions that had been deepening for decades. Mainstream commentators who wrote about these political divisions seemed to consistently blame conservatives for the discord. They rarely gave even a nod to the fact that conservatives were fighting a defensive battle to preserve their constitutional liberties.

America—an "Oppressor" Nation

A prime example of the myopic perspective of most political commentators was *The Second Civil War*, a book by veteran reporter Ronald Brownstein. Published in 2007, near the end of the Bush administration and ten years before the Trump era, Brownstein's book opens with a salvo against Tom DeLay, the former Republican House majority leader. DeLay was forced out of his leadership position and into retirement by a Democrat-engineered criminal prosecution. He was convicted of conspiracy to violate election laws, but the conviction was overturned years later—after his career and reputation had been ruined.

Brownstein seized on a line from what he snarkily called DeLay's "farewell address," in which he had advised his fellow Republicans, in passing, not to cooperate so much with their Democratic colleagues. This was probably because DeLay, like many others on the right, thought Republicans regularly got rolled when they did cooperate. But Brownstein cites DeLay's advice as a symptom of the "extreme partisanship" that had "paralyzed Washington and polarized America." Republicans were of course responsible.

Nowhere in the 484-page book does Brownstein refer to the 60-year aggression by the left against America's religious communities and America's founding principles. *Roe v. Wade* is mentioned exactly once, in passing, on p. 396. The term "religious liberty" is missing from its index.

The actual origins of America's current political divisions can be traced to the emergence of the radical left in the 1960s and the riot they staged at the 1968 Democratic Convention in Chicago. Police and National Guardsmen were forced to battle thousands of rioting members of such groups as the Youth International Party (Yippies), the Black Panthers, and Students for a Democratic Society. The fallout from this debacle destroyed the presidential hopes of Vice President Hubert Humphrey, a liberal whose sin was to have supported America's anti-Communist war in Vietnam.

Humphrey's defeat paved the way for radicals to move into the Democratic Party en masse, changing its structures and then its politics. Among the radicals' first achievements was the creation of congressional "caucuses" based on race, ethnicity, gender, and support for progressive causes. These caucuses provided the platforms from which they advanced their leftist agendas within the party, agendas focused on "identity politics" and making America the bad guy.

Over the next four years, the far-left radicals—led by Tom Hayden and Jane Fonda—marched into the Democratic Party and swept traditional liberalism away. They replaced it with a leftism that views American society as a system of oppressive hierarchies based on race, gender, and sexual orientation.

Leftists believe these hierarchies *must* be overthrown. Theirs is a collectivist ideology, rooted in Marxism, that is opposed to the American ideas of individual rights, individual accountability, and individual equality. By proposing that America oppresses races and genders, it is a politics that is blind to the opportunities and rights that America actually offers to all its citizens.

Labeling Political Opponents "Phobic"

The 2016 Democratic presidential campaign was a classic prosecution of these identity politics. Although the Democratic candidate, Hillary Clinton, had built her entire career on the political shoulders of her presidential husband, she framed her campaign as a movement against an imaginary "war on women." She claimed that an invisible patriarchal conspiracy held women down, keeping them oppressed beneath a "glass ceiling." Sexism—not her own shortcomings as a candidate—blocked her way to the top. These views were not exclusive to Hillary Clinton—these were now the core doctrines of the Democratic Party.

A seminal moment occurred during the 2016 presidential campaign when Hillary addressed an "LGBT for Hillary" fund-raising event. Speaking to the crowd of radical activists, she said, "You know, to just be grossly generalistic, you could put half of Trump's supporters into what I call the basket of deplorables. They're racist, sexist, homophobic, xenophobic—Islamophobic—you name it. . . . Now, some of those folks—they are irredeemable, but thankfully, they are not America."

This is a revealing statement. According to Hillary and her supporters, America is divided into two kinds of people. On the one hand there are *real* Americans who care about gay people, minorities, and other victim groups. On the other there are the Trump supporters, the un-American "deplorables" who hate and oppress society's victims.

This was a frank expression of the Democrats' hatred for their political opponents. It's also a major departure from traditional American values of tolerance, compromise, and respect for dissenting opinions. It exposes how the very language of the Democrats' politics is designed to dehumanize and delegitimize anyone who disagrees with its leftist agendas.

Stigmatizing one's opponent is a classic radical tactic. It is the thirteenth rule of Saul Alinsky's Rules for Radicals: "Pick the target, freeze it, personalize it, and polarize it."[3] Attack your opponents personally and cut them off from any possibility of sympathy. That is why radicals paint their political opponents as homophobes, xenophobes, and Islamophobes. They're not just good-but-misguided people whose religious convictions have led them to a contrasting viewpoint. They are *bad* people possessed by irrational fears of "the others" because they are different.

According to the left, in other words, people who oppose abortion and same-sex marriage have a kind of mental illness. They are not reasonable people, and their thoughts are not rational thoughts. These ritualistic indictments of the sanity of political opponents destroy the fabric of America's pluralism, which requires a respect for opposing views and a search for compromise. Calling critics "phobic" is a rationale for denying their First Amendment rights. Shouts of "No free speech for homophobes or Islamophobes" are already heard from leftists on college campuses. Or, to put them all in one fearful basket: "No free speech for fascists."

"Sexism" and "People of Color"

To erase individual features and circumstances, and to collectivize people into victim groups, the left employs ideological terms of art like "sexism" and "people of color." "Sexism" is a bastardized term coined by sixties' radicals in a calculated attempt to appropriate the moral authority of the civil rights movement. The goal is to place "sexism" on the same moral plane as "racism."

Only a perverse reading of history and the social relations between the sexes could lead to this offensive attempt to link the treatment of African Americans with attitudes toward women. But for radicals the conflation of the two is essential to their Marxist vision of society as a hierarchy of oppression.

Before the invention of the term "sexism," there were a multitude of adjectives to describe specific bad behaviors involving men and women: "inappropriate," "indecent," "rude," "boorish," "prejudiced," "offensive"—all the way to criminal behaviors such as molestation and rape. These adjectives describe a spectrum of behaviors with gradations from what is merely annoying to what is prosecutable. The term "sexism" erases these distinctions and obliterates nuances and individual circumstances by making all these behaviors instances of sexual oppression. Once the obliteration of specific detail takes place, "sexism" can even make a compliment—"My, you're good-looking"—appear to be an example of gender oppression, and prosecutable as such. An "inappropriate" or "offensive" remark might demonstrate poor judgment. But a "sexist" remark is a criminal injustice.

Differentiating between offensive behaviors, instead of subsuming them under the rubric "sexism," makes it possible to judge individual actions and motives on the way to arriving at a just remedy. But once these behaviors are grouped under a single term, the alleged "war against women" can begin to seem real. Because it is improper to put oppressor and oppressed on the same moral plane, we are no longer discussing a single instance of inappropriate behavior or a particular interaction in which the female may also share the blame. We are discussing the alleged general "oppression" of women by men. By obliterating the particulars and casting the parties as genders rather than individuals, the question of guilt and innocence is preordained.

The left has also coined the phrase "people of color" to facilitate its anti-white racism. Like "sexism," this term, too, has entered the general language. The phrase is not grammatical English; nor does it define a coherent group with a common social identity or interest. The Tutsis and Hutus of Rwanda are both people of color. But the Hutus carried out a genocide in which they massacred a million Tutsis. "People of color" is an ideological device whose sole purpose is to promote the idea that people of color are a group oppressed by the only people who are not "of color"—white people.

"People of color" obscures the fact that white majorities in America supported and, in fact, architected the Civil Rights Acts, and have helped to create a society in which black Americans have more rights and opportunities and privileges than blacks in any other country in the world, even those ruled by blacks. "People of color," with its implication that blacks are still oppressed, obscures the reality that the majority of blacks in America are successful as the result of choices freely made in a free society, while a smaller underclass of blacks have somehow not been able to take advantage of the same opportunities. In other words, "people of color" is a term designed to obscure the fact that people have choices regardless of color for which they are responsible. Bottom line: "people of color" is a racist term that should have no place in America's culture of equal rights. It is a term created by people who are at war with this culture.

These politically correct words and phrases are weapons in the war of "resistance" that Democrats have waged against Trump from the moment he gained traction as a political figure. Trump was never an ideological conservative. If he has an ideology, it is patriotism. During the campaign this was manifest in his concern about the state of his country, the short shrift it had been given in global trade deals, the trillions squandered in wars that resulted in no gain, the porous state of its borders and the precarious condition of its security. His campaign themes made his patriotism clear: *Make America prosperous again, make America safe again, make America strong again, make America great again.*

"Patriotism" is not a term of endearment to people on the left, to the globalist elites, or to Democrats generally, who have found it difficult since Korea to support America's wars against its enemies. The racial haters on the left, in the Democratic Party and the media generally, have twisted Trump's patriotism and condemned it as a jingoistic and bigoted bravado. Unable to attack patriotism directly,

Democrats attacked Trump's love of country by calling it "white nationalism" and "white supremacy," i.e., white racism. When he attempted to block—even temporarily—immigrants from a handful of terrorist countries, because their governments could not vet them, the left tarred him as "anti-immigrant" and racist. These extreme distortions of Trump's positions were relentlessly repeated as the core themes of the Democrats' resistance, all part of their capitulation to leftist hatred of America itself.

Yet it was precisely Trump's patriotism that attracted populist support for his candidacy. His genuine love for his country was a key factor in gaining the crucial support of evangelical Christians and Catholics. This coalition pushed Trump over the top in the Republican primaries, when other factions of the party remained skeptical. The same coalition stood strongly behind him through his victory in the general election.

Why the Religious Right Embraced Trump

To the left, the support Trump received from the religious right remained an insoluble mystery. He was thrice married, not particularly religious, and often vulgar and carrying some unsavory sexual baggage. He had supported abortions and gay marriage in the past. Yet evangelicals and Catholics cheered him at rallies, proudly wore Make America Great Again! hats, and pulled the lever for him at the polls.

The reason liberals didn't understand the religionists was because they had contempt for them, regarding them as bigoted and stupid. But anyone concerned about the half century of aggression that religious communities had suffered at the hands of the left could understand. Anyone who identified with the fight that conservatives waged in defense of religious liberty could understand. And anyone sympathetic to the unapologetic patriotism of religious people could understand why they were solidly for Trump, despite his flaws.

Tony Perkins, head of the Family Research Council, explained this phenomenon succinctly: "My support for Trump has never been based upon shared values; it is based upon shared concerns."[4] These shared concerns have made the religious right a crucial support not only for Trump but for American values and America's constitutional framework, which are under attack from its enemies within.

Instead of recognizing the way Trump's patriotic instincts resonated with the religious right, Democrats and their partisan media allies reached for the race card to discredit both. They concluded that evangelicals were attracted to Trump because of *racism*. "The media have been obsessed with *white* evangelicals' unmovable support for Donald Trump," an opinion piece in the *Washington Post* reported. "As a new poll from the Public Religion Research Institute shows, *white* evangelicals continue to be dedicated to Trump. His support among this group is at the highest levels ever, despite his alleged moral trespasses and lack of religious orientation" [emphasis added].

The writer goes on to explain: "My new book, *Immigrants, Evangelicals and Politics in an Era of Demographic Change*, shows *white* evangelicals are more conservative than other *whites* on policy issues including welfare, climate change and immigration. *Their conservative reaction to demographic change is at the heart of their political agenda and perhaps a response to increasing racial diversity within their own religious community*"[5] [emphases added].

This last point was a reference to the fact that 24 percent of the evangelical community is actually composed of minorities, whose views the leftist commentator had no intention of exploring. No evidence is given that white evangelicals are racists or that an aversion to demographic change is "at the heart" of the conservative political agenda. But in the rhetorical lexicon of the left, the only conceivable reason one could have for opposing radical politics—anti–free speech, open borders, anti-business, anti-military—is bigotry.

Evangelicals were ready to embrace Trump because he cared about America, and the principles behind America's greatness, which are Christian in origin. When Justice Antonin Scalia died in early 2016 and Trump promised to fill the vacancy with an "originalist" judge from a list provided by the conservative Federalist Society, the alliance between Trump and evangelicals was sealed. This promise reflected both Trump's concern for a community under attack and also his understanding that the same attacks imperiled America's social contract. Trump's determination to secure America's borders, and to brave the racist slurs that the "no-borders" Democrats hurled at him, was a sign of the patriotic passion that formed his political core.

Christians were also reassured by his combative nature, which indicated to all conservatives that the long night of weak Republican leadership and inadequate defense of the Republic was over. There was a new commander-in-chief at the helm, and he was going to defend their country and Constitution.

A Nation Divided

Trump's bold actions exposed just how extensively the anti-American left's influence had come to shape Democratic Party politics. Senator Kamala Harris is one of a handful of leading contenders for the 2020 Democratic presidential nomination. Like her colleagues, she is a supporter of racial preferences, a practitioner of racial politics, and an advocate of open borders. She opposed Trump's nomination of Neil Gorsuch to the Supreme Court on the grounds that "Judge Gorsuch has consistently valued legalisms over real lives."[6] In other words, if he were made a Supreme Court Justice, Gorsuch would value the Constitution over Harris's political prejudices.

When Justice Anthony Kennedy announced his retirement in Trump's second year, Democrats went into panic mode at the prospect that the new court might overturn *Roe v. Wade*. Kamala Harris said of Trump's appointee, D.C. Circuit Judge Brett Kavanaugh, "We're looking at the destruction of the Constitution."[7] This was the view of leftists who had no respect for the Constitution to begin with. For them, overturning an invented constitutional right as in *Roe v. Wade*, and allowing fifty diverse states to decide what is appropriate abortion policy for their people—which is what would happen if *Roe* were overturned—was "the destruction of the Constitution."

Speaking at a Howard University commencement in 2017, Harris urged her audience to join the Democrats' resistance to the Trump administration: "Graduates, indeed we have a fight ahead. This is a fight to define what kind of country we are, and it's a fight to determine what kind of country we will be." Ignore for a moment the impropriety of addressing a graduating class of students as though they were Democratic Party operatives. Instead, focus on the statement itself.

The call "to define what kind of country we are" is an ominous agenda for Americans. The Constitution already defines the kind of country we are. That document has served America well for over 200 years. It has made this nation a beacon of freedom for the entire world. America is unique among nations in having been *defined in its creation*. But redefining America is exactly what the radical left and the Democratic Party have been doing for the last fifty years.

It took a Civil War and 200 years of sacrifice and struggle to achieve a society that approaches the ideals laid down in our country's founding documents. That achievement is now endangered by a party committed to an identity politics that is the antithesis of the ideas and principles the founding established. Instead of cherishing religious liberty and individual freedom, the Democrats offer us a reversion to tribal loyalties and collectivist values. They regard immutable origins—skin colors, ethnicities, genders, and classes—as primary factors in judging individuals and determining what is just.

A nation divided by such fundamental ideas—individual freedom on one side and group identity on the other—cannot long endure, any more than could a nation that was half slave and half free. The urgency that drew the religious right into politics fifty years ago is now an urgency of the nation itself.

Endnotes

CHAPTER 1

1. https://en.wikipedia.org/wiki/Persecution_of_Christians_in_the
   _Soviet_Union.
2. https://en.wikipedia.org/wiki/Religulous.
3. Anna Salleh, "Are Religion and Science Always at Odds?," ABC
   Science (Australia), May 23, 2018, http://www.abc.net.au/news/
   science/2018-05-24/three-scientists-talk-about-how-their-faith-fits
   -with-their-work/9543772.
4. Richard Dawkins, *The God Delusion* (Boston: Mariner Book, 2006),
   Kindle edition, p. 308.
5. Ibid.
6. Carol Kuruvilla, "12 Famous Scientists on the Possibility of God,"
   Huffington Post, April 11, 2017, https://www.huffingtonpost.com/
   entry/12-famous-scientists-on-the-possibility-of-god_us_56afa292e
   4b057d7d7c7a1e5.
7. Time International, November 5, 2006, http://inters.org/Dawkins
   -Collins-Cray-Science.

8. Ibid.
9. Genesis 3:5 KJV.

CHAPTER 2

1. Christopher Hitchens, *God Is Not Great: How Religion Poisons Everything* (New York: Twelve/Hachette, 2007), p. 56.
2. Ibid., loc. 4040–4041.
3. David Horowitz, "The Two Christophers: Or, the Importance of Second Thoughts," in *Ruling Ideas*, Vol. IX of *The Black Book of the American Left*, 2018.
4. Blaise Pascal, *Pensees*, #205.
5. Ibid., #229.
6. Ibid., #278.
7. https://en.wikipedia.org/wiki/Blaise_Pascal.
8. Christopher Hitchens, *The Portable Atheist: Essential Readings for the Non-Believer* (Da Capo Press, 2007), Introduction.
9. Richard Alleyne and Mick Brown, "Atheist Christopher Hitchens Could Be 'Saved' by Evangelical Christian," *Telegraph* (UK), March 26, 2011, https://www.telegraph.co.uk/news/health/news/8407326/Atheist-Christopher-Hitchens-could-be-saved-by-evangelical-Christian.html.
10. Larry S. Taunton, *The Faith of Christopher Hitchens: The Restless Soul of the World's Most Notorious Atheist* (Nashville, TN: Nelson Books, 2016), Kindle edition, pp. 180, 181.
11. Hitchens, *The Portable Atheist*, loc. 395.
12. http://www.askatheists.com/7276.
13. I Corinthians 13:12.
14. Proverbs 16:18.

CHAPTER 3

1. Nicholas Humphrey, "What Shall We Tell the Children?," Amnesty Lecture, Oxford, February 21, 1997, https://www.edge.org/3rd_culture/humphrey/amnesty.html.
2. Richard Wurmbrand, *Tortured for Christ: The 50th Anniversary Edition* (Colorado Springs, CO: David C. Cook, 2017), pp. 151–152.
3. https://fatherstephen.wordpress.com/2008/08/04/solzhenitsyn-and-where-the-battle-begins/.

CHAPTER 4

1. James Rosen, "Conservative Lawmakers Bring God to Capitol Visitor Center," McClatchy Newspapers, December 2, 2008, https://www.mcclatchydc.com/news/politics-government/article24512779.html.
2. The actual quotation was "We have built no national temples but the Capitol; we consult no common oracle but the Constitution." From Samuel Gilman Brown, ed., *The Works of Rufus Choate with a Memoir of His Life* (Boston: Little, Brown, and Co., 1862), p. 345.
3. David Limbaugh, *Persecution: How Liberals Are Waging War against Christians* (Washington, D.C.: Regnery, 2003), Kindle edition, p. 302.
4. Mark David Hall, *Did America Have a Christian Founding?* Heritage Foundation, June 7, 2011, https://www.heritage.org/political-process/report/did-america-have-christian-founding.
5. Jon Meacham, *American Gospel: God, the Founding Fathers, and the Making of a Nation* (New York: Random House, 2006), p. 65.
6. Paul Leicester Ford, ed., *The Works of Thomas Jefferson*, Vol. 12 (New York: G. P. Putnam's Sons, 1905), p. 42.
7. *Federalist*, No. 51.
8. Meacham, op. cit., p.21.

CHAPTER 5

1. Alyssa Marsico, "Fla. 5-Year-Old Told 'It's Not Good' to Pray by School Employee," KDKA2 CBS Pittsburgh, April 1, 2014, https://pittsburgh.cbslocal.com/2014/04/01/florida-5-year-old-told-its-not-good-to-pray-by-school-employee/.
2. Liberty Institute, "10-Year-Old Shelby County School Student Finally Permitted to Write about Her Hero—God!," press release, October 17, 2013.
3. https://www.nbclosangeles.com/news/local/Student-Not-Allowed-Talk-About-Bible-School-Lawyer-240195351.html.
4. The opinion was written by Chief Judge Charles S. Desmond.
5. http://www.free2pray.info/2schoolprayerrulings.html.
6. https://www.freedomforuminstitute.org/2005/01/27/plaintiff-in-1962-landmark-school-prayer-case-reflects-on-his-role/.
7. Thomas Jefferson, "Letter to the Danbury Baptists—the Final Letter, as Sent," Library of Congress, *Information Bulletin*, June 1998, https://www.loc.gov/loc/lcib/9806/danpre.html.

8. https://en.wikipedia.org/wiki/Engel_v._Vitale.

9. David Limbaugh, *Persecution: How Liberals Are Waging War against Christians*, (Washington, D.C.: Regnery, 2003), Kindle edition. p. 25.

10. Fox News, "Founding Fathers, Classroom Lookism, and Standardizing the Tests, FoxNews.com, February 6, 2002, http://www.foxnews.com/story/2002/02/06/founding-fathers-classroom-lookism-and-standardizing-tests.html.

11. Paul Vitz, *Censorship: Evidence of Bias in Our Children's Textbooks* (Ann Arbor, MI: Servant, 1986), pp. 18–19, 65.

12. "Intro to Islam" https://www.youtube.com/watch?v=ZHujiWd4914; "5 Pillars," https://www.youtube.com/watch?v=ikVGwzVg48c.

13. Thomas More Law Center, "Chatham Middle School Students Are Taught That Islam Is the True Faith; Two Mothers Pilloried for Making It Public; Must See Video," ThomasMore.org, March 30, 2017, https://www.thomasmore.org/press-releases/chatham-middle-school-students-taught-islam-true-faith-two-mothers-pilloried-making-public-must-see-video/.

14. Staff, "Parents Concerned over Religious Curriculum," Columbia (TN) *Daily Herald*, September 3, 2015, http://www.columbiadailyherald.com/news/local-news/parents-concerned-over-religious-curriculum.

15. Joshua Gill, "Christian Parent Furious after School Instructs Children to Write Out Their Submission to Allah," *Daily Caller*, May 17, 2018, https://dailycaller.com/2018/05/17/west-virginia-christian-parent-school-submissions-to-allah/.

16. Paul Sperry, "Look Who's Teaching Johnny about Islam: Saudi-Funded Islamic Activists Have Final Say in Shaping Public-School Lessons on Religions," *WorldNetDaily*, May 3, 2004. Cited in Spencer, op. cit.

17. Ibid.

18. "Judge Rules Islamic education OK in California Classrooms," *WorldNetDaily*, December 13, 2003. Cited in Spencer, op. cit.

19. See David Horowitz, *Unholy Alliance: Radical Islam and the American Left* (Washington, D.C.: Regnery Books, 2004).

CHAPTER 6

1. http://www.free2pray.info/2schoolprayerrulings.html.

2. Ted Dracos, *UnGodly: The Passions, Torments, and Murder of Atheist Madalyn Murray O'Hair* (New York: Free Press, 2003), p. 59.

3. Madalyn Murray O'Hair, *An Atheist Epic* (Cranford, NJ: American Atheist Press, 1989), p. 39.
4. Dracos, op. cit., p. 31.
5. Ibid., p. 11.
6. Robert J. McKeever, *The United States Supreme Court: A Political and Legal Analysis* (New York: Manchester University Press, 1997), p. 34.
7. Dracos, op. cit., p. 37.
8. O'Hair, op. cit., p. 211.
9. Ibid., pp. 47–48.
10. William J. Murray, *My Life without God* (Washington, D.C.: WND Books, 2012), pp. 1–3.
11. Ibid., pp. 1–2.
12. Ibid., pp. 50–51.
13. Ibid.
14. Ibid., p. 89.
15. Ibid.
16. Ibid., p. 90.
17. *Playboy*, October 1965.

CHAPTER 7

1. Alan Sears and Craig Osten, *The ACLU vs. America* (Nashville, TN: Broadman & Holman, 2005), Kindle edition, p. 10.
2. Helena Huntington Smith, "They Were Eleven," *The New Yorker*, July 5, 1930, https://www.newyorker.com/magazine/1930/07/05/they-were-eleven.
3. Margaret Sanger, *Woman and the New Race*, 1916? Kindle edition, loc. 26.
4. Ibid., loc. 61.
5. Margaret Sanger, *The Pivot of Civilization*, 1922, Kindle edition, loc. 1536.
6. Ibid., loc. 1561.
7. Ibid.
8. For details on the development of this legal argument, see David J. Garrow, *Liberty and Sexuality, The Right to Privacy and the Making of Roe v. Wade* (Oakland: University of California Press, 1998), Kindle edition, esp. Chap. 4, "Creating the Right to Privacy."
9. https://www.law.cornell.edu/supremecourt/text/381/479#writing-USSC_CR_0381_0479_ZO.
10. Garrow, op. cit., p. 390.

11. Norma McCorvey, *Won by Love* (Nashville, TN: Thomas Nelson, 1997), p. 29.
12. Ibid., p. 30.
13. Roe, 410 U.S. at 153.
14. http://www.endroe.org/dissentsrehnquist.aspx.
15. *Yale Law Journal*, April 1973.
16. Ronald Reagan, Interview with Eleanor Clift, Jack Nelson, and Joel Havemann of the *Los Angeles Times*, June 23, 1986.
17. Robert Bork, *The Tempting of America: The Political Seduction of the Law* (New York: Touchstone, 1990), p. 292.
18. James Reston, "Washington, Kennedy and Bork," *New York Times*, July 5, 1987.
19. Cited in Bork, op. cit., p. 283.
20. Ibid., p. 299.
21. Ibid., pp. 287, 289.

CHAPTER 8

1. Helena Huntington Smith, "They Were Eleven," *The New Yorker*, July 5, 1930, https://www.newyorker.com/magazine/1930/07/05/they-were-eleven.
2. C-SPAN, American Life League News Conference, April 10, 1989, online video at https://www.c-span.org/video/standalone/?7052-1/pro-life-women-news-conference, transcribed by the author.
3. *Planned Parenthood v. Casey* 505 U.S. at 1002.
4. David J. Garrow, *Liberty and Sexuality: The Right to Privacy and the Making of Roe v. Wade* (Oakland: University of California Press, 1998), p. 617.
5. Michael Sean Winters, *Left at the Altar: How the Democrats Lost the Catholics and How the Catholics Can Save the Democrats* (New York: Basic Books, 2008), p. 113.
6. bid.
7. http://www.azquotes.com/author/7895-Florynce_Kennedy; Winters, op. cit., p. 130.
8. Winters, op. cit., p. 132.
9. Ibid., pp. 139–140.
10. Ibid., p. 139.
11. Ibid.; Daniel K. Williams, *Defenders of the Unborn: The Pro-Life Movement before Roe v. Wade* (New York: Oxford University Press, 2016), Kindle edition, pp. 8–9.

12. Phyllis Schlafly, *Who Killed the American Family* (Washington, D.C.: WND Books, 2014), p. 62.

13. Winters, op. cit., p. 118.

14. Michael Sean Winters, *God's Right Hand: How Jerry Falwell Made God a Republican and Baptized the American Right* (New York: HarperCollins, 2012), Kindle edition, p. 131.

15. Jerry Falwell, *Falwell: An Autobiography* (Tab Books, 1996), p. 388, https://en.wikipedia.org/wiki/Moral_Majority.

16. Winters, *God's Right Hand*, p. 110.

17. Jason L. Riley, "Let's Talk about the Black Abortion Rate," *Wall Street Journal*, July 10, 2018, https://www.wsj.com/articles/lets-talk-about-the-black-abortion-rate-1531263697; Timothy Dolan, "The Democrats Abandon Catholics," *Wall Street Journal*, March 22, 2018, https://www.wsj.com/articles/the-democrats-abandon-catholics-1521761348.

18. https://news.gallup.com/poll/163697/approve-marriage-blacks-whites.aspx.

19. Winters, *God's Right Hand*, p. 105; Falwell, *An Autobiography*, pp. 318–320.

CHAPTER 9

1. Mark Segal, "I Was at the Stonewall Riots. The Movie 'Stonewall' Gets Everything Wrong," PBS.org, September 23, 2015, https://www.pbs.org/newshour/arts/stonewall-movie.

2. "Gay Revolution Comes Out," *New York Rat Magazine*, August 12–26, 1969. The *Rat* was a publication put out by the Students for a Democratic Society.

3. Randy Shilts, *And the Band Played On* (New York: St. Martin's Press, 1987), Kindle edition, p. 19.

4. Ibid., p. 18.

5. https://en.wikipedia.org/wiki/Sex_Panic!.

6. Shilts, op. cit., p. 39.

7. Michael Callen, *Surviving AIDS* (New York: HarperCollins, 1990).

8. Ibid.

9. Shilts, op. cit., p. 39.

10. https://www.theroot.com/where-s-the-pride-in-pride-parades-1790869593.

11. http://thinkexist.com/quotation/aids_is_not_just_god-s_punishment_for_homosexuals/198214.html.

12. https://www.realclearpolitics.com/articles/2014/06/01/ronald_reagan_and_aids_correcting_the_record_122806.html.
13. Ibid.
14. My interview with gay activist Konstantin Berlandt.
15. Peter Collier and David Horowitz, "Whitewash," *California Magazine*, July 1983. Reprinted as "Origins of a Political Epidemic," in David Horowitz, *Culture Wars*, which is volume V of *The Black Book of the American Left* (Los Angeles: Second Thought Books, 2015).
16. My interview with Dr. Don Francis.
17. My interview with Dr. Mervyn Silverman.
18. Michael Warner, *The Trouble with Normal: Sex, Politics, and the Ethics of Queer Life* (New York: Free Press, 1999), p. 216.
19. https://en.wikipedia.org/wiki/Epidemiology_of_HIV/AIDS#United_States.
20. Shilts, op. cit., p. 246.
21. Collier and Horowitz, op. cit.
22. http://www.amfar.org/thirty-years-of-hiv/aids-snapshots-of-an-epidemic/.
23. Anthony M. Petro, *After the Wrath of God: AIDS, Sexuality, and American Religion* (New York: Oxford University Press, 2015), Kindle edition, p. 146.
24. Ibid., p. 133.
25. https://www.nytimes.com/1990/01/03/nyregion/rude-rash-effective-act-up-shifts-aids-policy.html.
26. https://nymag.com/daily/intelligencer/2018/02/we-all-live-on-campus-now.html.

CHAPTER 10

1. https://www.brainyquote.com/quotes/ronald_reagan_183965.
2. https://forums.catholic.com/t/saul-alinskys-book-rules-for-radicals-dedicated-to-lucifer/123873.
3. https://www.huffingtonpost.com/2008/06/03/obamas-nomination-victory_n_105028.html.
4. https://www.cnsnews.com/commentary/dr-paul-kengor/how-obama-made-good-his-promise-fundamentally-transform-united-states.
5. https://www.snopes.com/fact-check/saul-alinsky-dedicated-rules-for-radicals-to-lucifer/.

6. https://www.theguardian.com/world/2008/apr/14/barackobama
   .uselections2008.

7. https://www.heritage.org/europe/report/barack-obamas-top-10
   -apologies-how-the-president-has-humiliated-superpower.

8. Dinesh D'Souza, *Falwell before the Millennium: A Critical Biography*
   (Washington, D.C.: Regnery, 1984), p. 103.

9. https://www.theguardian.com/world/2009/mar/25/obama-war
   -terror-overseas-contingency-operations.

10. https://www.bloomberg.com/view/articles/2016-08-24/why-obama
    -let-iran-s-green-revolution-fail.

11. http://time.com/3453840/leon-panetta-iraqi-troop/.

12. https://www.washingtonpost.com/politics/obamas-speech-at-prayer
    -breakfast-called-offensive-to-christians/2015/02/05/6a15a240-ad50
    -11e4-ad71-7b9eba0f87d6_story.html?noredirect=on&utm_term
    =.9678866af952.

CHAPTER 11

1. Michael Weinstein, News Release: "MRFF Unveils General Teichert's
   Nefarious Fundamentalist Agenda, Igniting Media Coverage
   Internationally," Military Religious Freedom Foundation, August
   14, 2018, http://militaryreligiousfreedom.org/press-releases/2018/
   Teichert_August%2013_.html.

2. Eric Lichtblau, "Questions Raised Anew about Religion in Military,"
   New York Times, February 28, 2009, https://www.nytimes.com/2009/
   03/01/washington/01church.html.

3. Ibid.

4. Michael L. Weinstein, "Fundamentalist Christian Monsters: Papa's
   Got a Brand New Bag," *Huffington Post*, April 16, 2013, https://
   www.huffingtonpost.com/michael-l-weinstein/fundamentalist
   -christian-_b_3072651.html.

5. https://nymag.com/daily/intelligencer/2018/05/obamas-legacy
   -has-already-been-destroyed.html.

6. "Lack of Transparency Is a Huge Political Advantage," October 17,
   2013, https://www.youtube.com/watch?v=G790p0LcgbI; http://
   ldi.upenn.edu/ahec2013/agenda.

7. https://www.nationalreview.com/2016/03/little-sisters-poor
   -supreme-court/andhttps://www.askheritage.org/how-is-president
   -obama-attacking-religious-liberty/.

8. Ibid.

9. http://www.lifenews.com/2016/05/16/little-sisters-win-supreme
-court-tells-lower-courts-to-protect-them-from-hhs-mandate/.

10. https://www.theatlantic.com/politics/archive/2015/07/obama
-beats-the-nuns-on-contraception/398519/.

11. Ibid.

12. https://wallbuilders.com/americas-biblically-hostile-u-s-president/.

13. https://www.usnews.com/news/the-report/articles/2015/06/26/
supreme-court-victories-for-obama-gay-rights.

14. https://conservancy.umn.edu/bitstream/handle/11299/183100/
2%20-%20Graglia.pdf?sequence=1&isAllowed=y.

15. https://abcnews.go.com/US/baker-won-supreme-court-case
-maintains-cake-couple/story?id=55660012.

16. http://www.adfmedia.org/files/MasterpieceHearingTranscript.pdf.

17. https://abcnews.go.com/US/baker-won-supreme-court-case
-maintains-cake-couple/story?id=55660012.

18. https://www.nationalreview.com/2017/01/obama-administration
-has-troubled-religious-liberty-legacy/.

19. Ibid.

20. https://www.supremecourt.gov/opinions/12pdf/12-307_6j37.pdf.

21. https://www.speaker.gov/general/conscience-protection-act-what
-it-and-why-it-s-needed.

22. https://www.cleveland.com/metro/index.ssf/2016/07/house_passes
_conscience_protec.html.

23. https://prod-cdn-static.gop.com/static/home/data/platform.pdf.

CHAPTER 12

1. Gregory A. Smith and Jessica Martinez, "How the Faithful Voted: A
Preliminary 2016 Analysis," Pew Research, November 9, 2016, http://
www.pewresearch.org/fact-tank/2016/11/09/how-the-faithful-voted
-a-preliminary-2016-analysis/.

2. Katha Pollitt, "Why Evangelicals—Still!—Support Trump," *The
Nation*, March 22, 2018, https://www.thenation.com/article/why
-evangelicals-still-support-trump/.

3. Saul Alinsky, *Rules for Radicals* (New York: Vintage, 1989), p. 130.

4. Salena Zito and Brad Todd, *The Great Revolt: Inside the Populist Coalition
Reshaping American Politics* (New York: Crown Forum, 2018), p. 173.

5. https://www.washingtonpost.com/news/monkey-cage/wp/2018/06/
19/white-evangelicals-still-support-donald-trump-because-theyre

-more-conservative-than-other-evangelica http://insider.foxnews
.com/2018/06/29/kamala-harris-rips-trump-supreme-court
-destruction-constitution-coming ls-this-is-why/?utm_term=
.fe129c70a1e6.

6. http://www.discoverthenetworks.org/individualProfile.asp?indid
-2760.

7. http://insider.foxnews.com/2018/06/29/kamala-harris-rips-trump
-supreme-court-destruction-constitution-coming.

Index

About the Author

D AVID HOROWITZ BEGAN HIS literary career 56 years ago with a book about student protests at Berkeley. He is the author of the most widely praised autobiographies of the sixties—*Radical Son: A Generational Odyssey*, which recounts his childhood in a Communist household, his role as one of the founders of the New Left and editor of its largest magazine, *Ramparts*, to his transformation into one of the nation's most important conservative intellectuals. Of him, the feminist writer Camille Paglia once said: "I respect the astute and rigorously unsentimental David Horowitz as one of America's most original and courageous political analysts. He has the true 1960s spirit—audacious and irreverent, yet passionately engaged and committed to social change. As a scholar who regularly surveys archival material, I think that, a century from now, cultural historians will find David Horowitz's spiritual and political odyssey paradigmatic for our time."

After leaving the left, Horowitz co-authored three generational biographies with Peter Collier, *The Rockefellers: An American Dynasty, The*

Kennedys: An American Drama, and *The Fords: An American Epic*. The *Rockefellers* and *The Kennedys* were *New York Times* best-sellers, *The Kennedys* occupying number one on the *Times'* list 7 weeks in a row.

In 1999, Horowitz published *Hating Whitey & Other Progressive Causes*, the first of three books he was to write on the subject of race. In 2001, he published *Uncivil Wars: The Controversy Over Reparations for Slavery*, a narrative of his campaign to oppose reparations for slavery as a misguided effort to divide a nation which had led the world in abolishing slavery and had reached a point where any program proven to help disadvantaged African Americans would have overwhelming bi-partisan support. These books were prescient accounts of the growing influence of "identity politics"—a form of cultural Marxism—on the Democratic Party and the left generally.

In 2004, Horowitz published another path-breaking work, *Unholy Alliance: Radical Islam and the American Left*, which set out to explain how self-regarding liberals and progressives could form a tacit alliance with a barbarous ideology that was misogynistic, bigoted and totalitarian, and determined to destroy the United States.

Horowitz saw the root of these anti-American ideologies as lying in the transformation of American universities—or more specifically their liberal arts divisions into indoctrination and recruitment centers for the political left. Horowitz documented these claims and explained how the transformation took place, in a series of books beginning with *The Professors* (2005), and including *Indoctrination U.* (2007), *One-Party Classroom* (2009), and *Reforming Our Universities* (2010).

Horowitz then turned from polemical and political writings to a genre that was autobiographical and philosophical, publishing a trilogy of lyrical works that included *The End of Time* (2005), *A Point In Time* (2011), and *You're Going To Be Dead One Day: A Love Story* (2015). Of the first of this series, the critic Stanley Fish commented: "Beautifully written, unflinching in its contemplation of the abyss, and yet finally hopeful in its acceptance of human finitude," while Walter Isaacson described it as "a poignant and powerful rumination on the meaning of life and the meaning of death." Similar encomiums were offered for the subsequent volumes. "David Horowitz is so powerful a polemicist that it is often forgotten how beautifully he writes," Norman Podhoretz observed of *A*

Point In Time, "this little book boldly ventures into an exploration of first things and last that is as moving as it is profound.

During the period of writing these books, tragedy struck the author, as his oldest daughter died of a congenital disease at the age of 43. An amazing and profound individual, her death inspired one of the most moving elegies of our time in a book called, *A Cracking of the Heart* (2009).

While he was writing these meditative books, Horowitz was hard at work forming his voluminous writings about the left into a 9-volume series, which he called *The Black Book of the American Left,* and which he completed in 2018. The volumes are organized by subject matter *1. My Life & Times, 2. Progressives, 3. The Great Betrayal, 4. Islamo-Fascism & the War Against the Jews, 5. Culture Wars, 6. Progressive Racism, 7. The Left in the Universities, 8. The Left in Power,* and *9. Ruling Ideas.* Of the series, the author Bruce Bawer has said, "If there were any justice, these volumes—which began coming out in 2013—would be widely recognized as definitive studies of the politics of modern American life."

In addition to the Black Book series, Horowitz has recently written *Radicals: Portraits of a Destructive Passion* (2012), *Take No Prisoners: The Battle Plan for Defeating the Left* (2014), and *Big Agenda: President Trump's Plan to Save America* (2017), which was on the *New York Times* bestseller list for 11 weeks in a row.

Simple **Heart Test**

Powered by Newsmaxhealth.com

FACT:

▶ Nearly half of those who die from heart attacks each year never showed prior symptoms of heart disease.

▶ If you suffer cardiac arrest outside of a hospital, you have just a 7% chance of survival.

Don't be caught off guard. Know your risk now.

TAKE THE TEST NOW ...

Renowned cardiologist **Dr. Chauncey Crandall** has partnered with **Newsmaxhealth.com** to create a simple, easy-to-complete, online test that will help you understand your heart attack risk factors. Dr. Crandall is the author of the #1 best-seller *The Simple Heart Cure: The 90-Day Program to Stop and Reverse Heart Disease.*

Take Dr. Crandall's Simple Heart Test — it takes just 2 minutes or less to complete — it could save your life!

Discover your risk now.

- **Where you score on our unique heart disease risk scale**
- Which of your lifestyle habits really protect your heart
- **The true role your height and weight play in heart attack risk**
- Little-known conditions that impact heart health
- **Plus much more!**

SimpleHeartTest.com/Agenda

CPSIA information can be obtained
at www.ICGtesting.com
Printed in the USA
BVHW041412130621
609030BV00015B/15/J